ONE ROSE IN BALI

HILARY ROOTS

ETT IMPRINT

ExileBay

This Imprint Classics edition published by ETT Imprint in 2026

First published by ETT Imprint, Exile Bay in 2022
First ebook edition published by ETT Imprint in 2025

Copyright © Hilary Roots 2022

This book is copyright. Apart from any fair dealing for the purposes of private study, research, criticism or review, as permitted under the Copyright Act, no part may be reproduced by any process without written permission. Enquiries should be addressed to the publisher, or via this email ettimprint@hotmail.com

ETT IMPRINT
PO Box R1906
Royal Exchange NSW 1225
Australia

ISBN 978-1-923527-16-4 (paper)
ISBN 978-1-922698-67-4 (ebook)

Cover design Tom Thompson
Cover photograph by Albert

CONTENTS

1. The man in white 5
2. Where do you go when you go to sleep? 13
3. The end - just the beginning 24
4. Waiting for an auspicious day 29
5. ... and on the 5th day 37
6. White sand, warm sun, French food... 50
7. A rose 53
8. Swiss national colours 59
9. Swirling waters of widowhood 65
10. A designer life 68
11. Officialdom: Beware, be wary 80
12. Unexpected kindnesses 91
13. A new year - and yet, a closing 96
14. Melodies 99
15. Trees and memories 102
16. More roses 107
17. In praise of the iPad 111
18. Days ahead 113
    Reference Works 115

ONE

The man in white

His hands are blue!

No oxygen is making its way there, gasps Ketut, prising open Albert's age and weather-speckled, long-fingered artist's hands.

It's a bad sign, that's sure.

What can we do? I beg, dumb-founded. He needs to go to hospital.

But Ketut, we can't move Albert.

A big man – 1 metre 83 cm, some 105 kilos, unable to sit, unable to stand. We just cannot move him.

Albert starts to breathe more heavily, as if trying to catch his breath. His chest is heaving. Oh I wish I could calm him, that I could help him.

Ketut rushes away. He goes to make phone calls. He tries one, two, three doctors – they all reply, in a while, in an hour. Then he has a flash; he remembers he has a friend in charge of an Ubud emergency clinic. He calls him for help. And, it works. Help arrives in lightning time. It seems only minutes. We girth Albert with a *paréo/sarong*. In the tropics you wear nothing between the sheets. I'm lightly clad for early morning, not exactly respectable for going out on the street, but I don't think about that. My head and heart race. I gather up papers, copies of passports and travel insurance. Suddenly, beside our bed are stretcher-bearers, oxygen and, after a hustle down the garden path, an ambulance. We run.

The ambulance siren clears a passage to the clinic on the outskirts of town. It's a ride that takes perhaps 10 minutes, but seems interminable, frightening, into the unknown.

Manoeuvring a tall, heavy body is not an easy task, but there are numerous helpers and they manage to haul the stretcher up several steps on to an open examination podium. A young doctor heading the emergency team checks Albert over. He impresses me with his efficiency. We must go to hospital. So back down the steps and into the ambulance again. Albert is masked up, strapped on, the oxygen flowing. He has two male nurses with him. I'm again in front with the driver. For the next 20 fast minutes of sirens and hooters, I keep turning round, looking back to see if Albert is alright. Toot toot, toot, toot. It seems we're in a film ride. We turn into a low-rise, new hospital in the countryside. Kasih Ibu, Saba.

Immediately, just inside the door, a team takes over, attending to Albert. A young female doctor examines him, while the doctor in charge questions me at the desk just across the open passage. He gives me his card: Dr Y. Primly dressed in refined, Balinese Ikat weave, cobalt-blue shirt, he informs me Albert's heart is failing after battling, throbbing earlier this morning. His lungs have fluid on them. His oxygen is dangerously low. My poor Albert. I keep an eye out from a distance. He lifts his head. He's fighting. Bewildered. I'm sure he wonders where he is. Where I am. Dr Y says I can be with him. I hasten to his side with Ketut. He takes Ketut's arm and manages "Be good". To me, he winks! Never has a tiny gesture meant so much. 'Twas the briefest swansong.

It wasn't meant to be this way. We'd come to Bali, enamoured as always with its charms.

Warm, sweet smells of Bali, wafts of nostalgia....
were the first words that tumbled from my pen on returning to the Hindu island just south of the Equator. Whiffs of floral perfumes and incense had cloaked us in the warm, humid air that characterises this land as we stepped forth at Ngurah Rai airport. It was a Sunday afternoon, mid-June. Absent were the hassle and hustlers we remembered from previous visits. Gone were the cool season's chills further south, in Australia and New Caledonia, at least for nine days.

Our friend and driver, Ketut, was there to meet us. He, slight, swarthy, svelte, darting brown eyes, sleek black hair, his unchanged allure belying his probably 40-plus years. We – we were easy to find. Albert tall, straight, always the man in white, from hat to toe, including his below-the-collar, wavy hair. Me – a give-away English/Irish freckle face, much the same height as Ketut – a minimalist, 1 metre 63 cm. Wide smiles, hugs. Welcome to Bali. Welcome home.

Swathes of new roads skirted Denpasar, the un-enticing island capital. Leading past Sanur, giant kites so emblematic of Bali flew metres long, horizontally, as if huge banners reached out to greet us. It was a faster road to semi-rural, hill-country, artsy Ubud; under an hour, to the small, cottage hotel we'd frequented over the years, going back to 1994.

There were familiar faces – Gusti, Ayu, Dana – staff we recognised and who recognised us. Yes, there was a comfortable sense of arriving home.

We'd asked for our preferred bungalow across a little bridge, at the end of the garden. We lay on the four-poster bed, watched the late afternoon light play on the carved, bronze-encrusted posts hung with gauze netting, and sighed. Here we are, to do nothing. Read our books. Swim, dine, literally take it easy. How wonderful. We've been to Bali, the Hindu island of otherwise Muslim Indonesia, a number of times since Albert turned 60. We've visited the north, the south, neighbouring Lembongan island with the family from Switzerland for the men to dive and for us, all six, to luxuriate in sifting sand through our toes for five days. We've hiked to the island's sacred centre, and stayed overnight on the edge of the active volcano, Agung, bathing in its natural heated pools. We've visited tea plantations and rice-fields, jewellery-makers and textile weavers, assisted at dance, music and shadow-puppet shows provided for tourists, and attended a cooking school in Benoa.

Adept at manipulating an iPod, the day after our arrival, Albert strolled round the garden taking pleasure in putting together a few photos to accompany the pithy message he sent to a number of friends: *Safely arrived in our little paradise where we savour each minute. Love & kisses, Al and Cleo.*

Odd, one might say, that he would call the spot "our little paradise", when most people look enviously at where we live in New Caledonia and, almost without exception, call it a paradise. Indeed, earlier in the year, a French overseas territories documentary team had filmed us at home in the garden. Albert's reply to: "Did he expect to see out his days on Isle of Pines?" "If the next 'paradise' is as good as this one, then yes."

Foreboding words? For little were we to know, he would be called to that next "paradise" in the short months that followed.

Until then, our particular "paradise" for more than four decades together had been a dot in the south-western Pacific Ocean. An island almost astride the Tropic of Capricorn, 65 km in circumference, home to just 2000 people. It's an island renown for its natural beauty, stunning, fine white sand beaches, luxuriant sub-tropical vegetation, clear, coral waters and a two-seasons climate – warm and cool.

Odd then, one might say, that Albert would describe the spot we'd come to on holiday, as "our little paradise".

"Cleo" he'd signed his message, using the name he gave me 42 years ago when I first came to live on Isle of Pines. Why? Because French people can't quite cope with my real first name, Hilary. Firstly, French speakers don't pronounce an "H", so the sound comes out as 'Ilary'. Then, when said that way it sounds like "*il a ri*", which means, he laughed. So then they, the French speakers, say "What a funny name!". We would explain that it's the equivalent of "Hilaire" or "Hilarion" (which happened to be the name of the island's High Chief). Their riposte: "But that's a man's name"; to which we'd reply: "Yes, but Hilary is the feminine."

After such a long-winded explanation, Albert felt there was no way we could live in a French context, with a name needing five minutes' explanation. So he decided to change it. Why "Cleo"? or "*Cléo*" in French? I'd worked as a radio and television journalist. I was blondish at the time and sported a Cleopatra-style haircut. (See photo of me in blue with Albert, Christmas 1976.) This reminded him of a film by Agnès Varda – *Cléo de 5 à 7*. That's it. Cléo. From now on you're Cléo – and Cléo I've stayed ever since.

Albert had attached several photos to accompany his arrival message. A designer, to the point where his maxim was "I think with my hands", he was enchanted by the hotel restaurant's table decorations: molten glass poured over a sinuous coffee plant root to make a slim vase holding just one pink anthurium or "boy flower". Living in a country not unfamiliar to coffee bushes, neither of us had ever contemplated the beauty of a coffee root. Albert toyed with the idea of bringing one of these decorations home, but hesitated, knowing the difficulty transporting vegetal products from one country to another. Instead, he satisfied himself with photographing it in the warm breakfast light. He then caught the soft light on a cascade of white, trumpet-like flowers looking from the hotel's entrance towards the multiplicity of workers' scooters parked neatly on the roadside opposite. Back inside the garden, his eye fell on the tall, coconut palm silhouettes reflected in the still, duck-egg blue of the generous pool. Come evening, when we headed for a drink and dinner in the same hotel restaurant, Albert was appeased by the statue of Buddha in prayer, and then snapped me peeping around the same cascade of white flowers, of which no-one knew the name, but which I've since discovered carry the latin nomenclature *Thunbergia grandiflora Alba*, in Indonesian, *Bunga Kelinci* and in English, *Bengal trumpet*. A species native to India, as the latter name suggests, the vine is considered a weed in Australia!

Back to Albert's photos. During the day, he'd captured Ketut and me out on the street, again in front of the *Bunga Kelinci* that he, Ketut, had planted two years earlier. For 25 years, our Balinese friend had been employed at the same hotel, working every morning from 6 to 8 in the garden – to the point it had become almost his garden. Ingenious – he'd put together a mini lawnmower from discarded washing-machine parts, to which he'd attached an electric cord, thus cutting neat patches of grass with little noise and inconvenience; he'd moved plants around, watched them grow, encouraged other employees to love the work, before taking on their regular hotel duties in whatever domain. Ketut's work after 8 a.m. was a driver – long trips to and from Denpasar airport, or on day trips accompanying visitors to the numerous tourist attractions all over mid-eastern Bali.

The photo of the praying Buddha bedecked with red hibiscus, Albert posted to his daughter in Switzerland, Béa, his only child, with an even pithier accompanying note: "Let the light guide you?". It was to be his last. Nothing presaged what was to follow.

Oddly, we'd changed bungalows. Not that we didn't like our first choice. But Monday morning turned out to be so different from our quiet Sunday arrival. It was back to work and, to our disappointment, renovation work was afoot with great gusto on the bungalow, or cottage as it's now called, next to ours. Walls were coming down, banging and sawing broke the calm and, as we were staying nine days, Albert insisted we couldn't put up with such disturbance to the peace we were seeking. So, yes, reception agreed to give us another – bigger, a modernised bathroom, closer to the pool and, as it turned out, more practical – although none of that we envisaged.

Tuesday, Albert was a bit tired and coughed a bit too. We put it down to the plane trip from Brisbane having been extremely cold. We bought some cough mixture and thought nothing more. Apart from a trip to the post office with Ketut to send home a pack of fine cotton shirts he'd had made in Gianyar, he rested. I wandered along Monkey Forest Road, more out of curiosity than anything else, and bought a couple of gifts. Otherwise, we stayed within the hotel. Wednesday, Albert was still tired and come evening he faltered a little on walking to the restaurant and ate almost nothing – completely out of character. Again, we still didn't worry.

However, that night, the night of June 21st, the longest night and shortest day in the Southern Hemisphere, I woke to hear Albert breathing in a strange, sporadic way. It seemed he couldn't catch his breath. Surreptitiously I slipped open my iPad and checked on hyperventilation. Accompany the patient and try to encourage calmer, slower breathing. So that's what I did; evoking all his years of being a diver and his having practised yoga too. I breathed in and out, slowly, repetitively, cradling his ample body to calm him and help restore his breathing. But no. He said he couldn't. Frequently he went to the toilet and, at one moment, I remember, I must have said something like we'll see in a few days, and I heard him mutter, "Anyway, this is the last". I didn't understand. The night wore on and on, the longest night indeed and, eventually, I must have dropped off to sleep, not realising there was such urgency.

Come Thursday morning, I woke early and hastened to the restaurant asking for a light breakfast to take to Albert, as he had not eaten more than a spoonful the night before. I returned 15 minutes later with a small, ham omelette and toast. But all was not right. Albert couldn't stand. He couldn't sit. I called Ketut. Help! He came quickly from close by in the garden. Albert. Albert. Come, we'll help you to the table outside to eat a bit. But it wasn't any good. Really Albert could neither sit nor stand. So we helped him lie down. I know not for what reason, but Ketut opens up Albert's hands – they're blue! No oxygen is making its way there.

Sometime, someday I'll ask the doctors, a doctor, my sister who's a pathologist, what all those symptoms meant. How I could have read them differently, perhaps understood more? At the time of writing, I'm still too fragile to broach the depth of details.

Puzzling too, after Albert's having had an "All OK" from a specialist cardiology check-up just two days before our trip. A fillip. We'd set off on our travels, dare I say, light-hearted.

I returned alone to our hotel following the upheaval of the previous long night and ensuing day, I sat in the hotel's open-air restaurant, reflecting on having left Albert in intensive care to set his heart right. I took out my iPad beside the shrub-surrounded, fountain pond. Here's what I jotted down:

> What is this pump
> that keeps on pumping
> water in the fountain
> day in, day out,
> month in, month out?
> And what are we but walking pumps,
> unaware, unconscious
> of the elaborate mechanism
> that gives us life-blood

Till the day it falters,
heaves as if hyper-ventilating,
leaves us staggering, breathless,
devoid of colour, of speech,
perhaps of life.

Spontaneous lines. I didn't think for a moment premonitory.

Footnote: The British Heart Foundation explains that the human heart beats around 100,000 times a day. This extraordinary, involuntary pump of which we are so rarely consciously aware, continuously moves about 5 litres of blood through our circulatory system.

TWO

Where do you go when you go to sleep?

The doctors decide to put Albert into intensive care straight away. Ketut and I accompany him on the stretcher in the stretcher-sized lift, up two floors. Behind the blue door, he's sedated, heavily, into an induced coma. For how long? I ask. Three to five days, comes the reply – we'll see.

How weird. We are to leave our dear Albert here, in those professional hands. From the glassed-in visitors' waiting area, our backs to the ward, beyond fields and coconut trees, sparse buildings, we glimpse the sea on the horizon – Saba by the sea, the Bali Sea. I say to Ketut Albert will be happy to see that when he wakes up. He'll also appreciate that this is a new hospital, pastel colours, attractive décor, and, importantly, no stomach-turning ammonia-like smell – a smell he always shied away from having lost his sister and close friend, two years older than him, when he was ten at Christmas-time during the War. Béatrice died of peritonitis before the availability of penicillin. That haunting memory was one reason we rarely spoke about death, our deaths, how we would confront it/them.

The way back to Ubud, driving at normal speed and not the break-neck, cut-through-all-in-sight ambulance rate, took, naturally, twice as long, some forty minutes in fact. The hospital in the countryside was a world away from the zing of tourist-laden Ubud. I return to Ubud Inn, a zombie. Ketut too was shaken. We rendezvous for tomorrow.

Come evening, I ask the staff for an oil candle to put on our terrace table. I find Albert's lighter, but, not being a smoker, have great difficulty using it, and burn the tip of my finger instead. Albert would have chuckled. Still I persist and decide I'll go the whole way. I remember we have a small bottle of gin in our fridge. I pour myself a tiny, neat gin – not unusual for me, and light myself one of his Davidoff cigarillos to which he's partial at aperitif time. I take a couple of puffs only, but that's enough for me to tell myself, Albert would totally approve. He's with me.

Friday 23 June 2017. I wake to a blur of a beautiful day. I send emails to family and friends...... Breakfast. Then Ketut drives me to Saba. This time I see the countryside – cornfields and sugar cane, newly planted rice fields, flower nurseries, a cock-fighting crowd, folk outside the tourism circuit, leading their normal working and playing lives. It's school holidays for the one month of the year. Children ride with their dogs perched on their bikes, others fly kites – Bali's traditional pastime for young and old, source of amusement, inspiration and creativity.

And Albert? I push the buzzer and am admitted to the intensive care ward. Of eight beds, only two are occupied. I meet two specialists. One, the anaesthetist from yesterday, a tall, handsome, modern looking man, his first name written I Gusti, denoting a high class Balinese. The other, a petite, seven-months pregnant, internal organs specialist. They both speak clear, understandable English. Later on I see that much of the reference material they consult on Internet is in English. Albert lies quietly. His eyes as if sealed. He's warm. He has tubes in his mouth and his nose. The woman specialist is not overly encouraging. "I'll be here again tomorrow. Come earlier", she says. "We'll continue the heavy antibiotic treatment for the *cellulitis.*" It's the first time I've heard this verdict. Has what we'd taken to be poor circulation in his legs really been an insidious infection that perhaps caused his legs to swell, and so spread from his legs to his lungs? "We'll do what we can", she states matter-of-factly. And so Ketut and I return to Ubud feeling nebulous, knowing nothing, simply hanging in mid-air.

That night I participate in an unusual event – a winter solstice-cum-new moon, healing, fire and gong bath in a replica of the Giza Pyramids. I'd read about it earlier in the week in an Ubud Life "what's on this month" magazine. Albert was as intrigued as I, especially as we'd been to Giza after a boat trip along the Nile, so I'd booked for us to attend. His unexpectedly being in hospital seemed all the more reason for me to continue, representing both of us, so to speak, having a different experience to tell him about and share with him later. I'd bring him here to visit when he was out of hospital. The convivial Pyramids gathering, several kilometres from Ubud centre, is in a clearing on a tree-surrounded rise. As night falls we're invited to make a great circle round a fire, toss a smidgen of sawdust and presumably our wish into the fire and listen to a white-clad guru chant in an unrecognisable tongue. The Southern Cross is clear above, frogs croak, cicadas trill, the air is warm – soothing. We're then invited to lie on one of the dozens of comfortable mattresses inside the dim hush of one of the titanium pyramids. I choose a far corner, alone with the gongs, bells, chimes, wooden rattles and the hum of a didgeridoo that resonate through my body. The session lasts about an hour. I concentrate on sending the healing energies to Albert. Please God make him well.

Refined, tasty food shared by some eighty participants, completes the evening. I strike up conversation with two younger people – Prabodhi, meaning enlightenment in Sanskrit, from Southern Taiwan, and Theodore, a 30 year-old Bulgarian from Arizona. I also briefly meet the owners and founders, an Australian/English couple from Perth. Four years earlier he'd had a vision and this April realised their extraordinary exploit, after having run a meditation centre in Western Australia for 10 years. Now they attract visitors from afar to catch a wash of their "Gong Bath". The evening wasn't wasted.

Albert get well, I pray.

Saturday 24 June. I rise in the cool quiet of early morn and do my yoga on the wooden floor. A fresh, tranquil breakfast follows – just-made fruit juice, a banana-coconut honey-drizzled pancake, I've always liked at Ubud Inn, and tea. Ketut and I set off at 9.30 for Saba.

Dr Y says maybe the tubes can come off this afternoon. He proves too optimistic. The accounts people want their bills paid. The ambulance and emergency clinic need to be settled too. Reality is there. It comes to haunt me, hassle me, every time I set foot in Kasih Ibu Hospital. As with any business run efficiently, accounts is the nerve hub of the affair. Here it's no different. Even physically, it's starkly confronting, set in-between the admittance, emergency area and the wards. Despite having international travel insurance, I'm hit by their bold refusal to pay on my behalf. I pay. They'll settle later. Three months later I'm still waiting. A year later I'm still waiting!

But the important reason for my being here in the sparkling, new, private hospital is: how is Albert?

Behind the blue door upstairs, hands washed, mask on, we all alike, nurses too, the tall, gentle anaesthetist takes his time to explain to me how Albert is. He has better oxygen (92 percent), better, clearer lungs than on Thursday when he was admitted. But there are still some whitish signs of water and infection. ARDS he writes down for me: Acute Respiratory Distress Syndrome.

I spend time with Albert. The light is quite bright, but his eyes continue sealed. Just his breathing is easy. His temperature lower than yesterday. His shoulder is warm and soft to lay and keep my hand on. I kiss and caress his brow. I'm with you. Stay with us, I whisper.

Only then I notice they've shaved some of his beard. A long while passes before the pregnant, specialist doctor arrives. I have time to chat with Dr M about our life, where we live, that Albert, at 83, still works six days a week. That he always has projects. Together we bring up the website Albert, I and a webmaster friend in France, provide as volunteers, for all Isle of Pines – www.isle-of-pines.com . I find the activities page and show him Albert, smiling, his shirt smattered in paint, brush in hand, in his workshop. This reveals a more human link with the interested doctor. Albert is not just a patient, cast into a sleeping world. He's a dynamic, creative man, still full of projects. Dr M's colleague arrives. Fresher, more smiling than yesterday, she checks all the information on Albert. The infection is a bit less than yesterday. His temperature lower. We'll do another Doppler scan tomorrow. A Doppler scan measures the amount of blood flow through the arteries and veins. Come late in the afternoon.

I leave him in watchful, competent hands, all working to bring him back again, to counter the failure and infection. Ketut waits patiently till after midday, cigarette after cigarette outside. We drive "home" along roads less congested than the previous days. The Emergency Clinic gives me the receipt for 2,17 million rupiah, roughly the equivalent of $A217.

It's the beginning of millions of rupiah we're solicited for over the following days, weeks.

Back at the hotel: *Terimah Kassi Ketut* – thankyou. He hugs me – till tomorrow.

The hotel's varied menu restaurant in a pleasant setting between the busy roadside and a quiet pond makes it comfortable and easy for me to eat there almost all the time. What shall I have for a late lunch today? Jaya, the friendly, genuinely concerned restaurant manager who got on well in a cheery way with Albert right from our arrival, suggests a "sandwich". The pale green bun filled with grilled tuna, tomato, avocado, accompanied by French fries and mayonnaise, makes for a holiday feeling. Thanks for the fun suggestion.

Late afternoon I have a swim. I'm all alone in the pool. It's as if I'm back home at midday, on our extraordinary Kuto beach – more than a kilometre of fine, white sand bordering one of the most beautiful and often empty beaches in the Pacific.

The day's going down. Albert would have turned on The Jazz Groove, an Internet jazz radio operating out of San Francisco, that we're fond of. So I find the same music on his iPod, take a drop of gin, a few puffs on one of his cigarillos and sit on the flower-fringed terrace. Again, I do as Albert would do. He's with me. And fortuitously, at Brisbane Airport I'd bought an absorbing book, *Understory*, by Dr Inga Simpson, a book about trees in sub-tropical Queensland. I was pleased to have its company.

Heeding Ketut's advice to also look after myself, I decide on a massage that same evening. The traditional Balinese, full body massage lasts about an hour. It's relaxing therapy worth every cent of the modest 18 Australian dollars. It begins with a courteous welcome: a cool, moist towel and a tamarillo juice. A first for me as a juice, yet the very mention of it, the rich burgundy colour, the distinctive odour and slightly tart taste send my mind whizzing to when I was a little girl staying with my grandparents in Patea, New Zealand. My grandfather grew what were then called "tree tomatoes" and my grandmother used to stew them. I loved them. I tell the receptionist the story. She tells me the spa owner's family is in Bedugul in the Bali Central Highlands. At 700 metres altitude they grow cooler climate produce and each day fresh fruit arrives in Ubud for them to make juice. I'm relaxing already.

My masseuse, Noli, is impressively strong in relation to her diminutive size. She pummels me for an hour with frangipani-infused oil. I float back to the hotel, just steps away. After such care and relaxation I opt for just a soup, then fall into a deep sleep, the way Albert is sleeping too.

Sunday 25 June. Our schedule is different today. Mid-day, I walk to a Japanese restaurant in the street parallel. Familiar food in a half open-air restaurant, where light rain falls in between the covered areas, is soothing. I'm to meet Ketut in the afternoon. He arrives at the hotel on his scooter, telling me to hop on behind. There's too much traffic in centre Ubud. It'll take us an hour to get out of the congested, narrow streets by car. So hop on, I do. This is Bali style: we ride against the traffic, between the gutter and the vehicles! No helmet, sandals, a wet road! I pray and hang on tightly to Ketut, he remarks later. In another situation I would have refused to embark on such a dangerous ride. But motivated by saving Albert, bringing him back to life and home fit and well, I accept to go the madcap kilometre or so to pick up Ketut's car near his home. He's not only someone we've known a little for 23 years, but now, each day our driving some 30 to 40 minutes to the country-side together, and our mission to save Albert, start to bring us close, he's becoming a bit like a brother, instead of a driver. He has time to tell me stories. Ten years ago, he tells me, he was in a car accident, resulting in his being in a true coma for 22 days! His story reassures me that Albert could come out of his coma – perhaps today? Perhaps tomorrow? We arrive late in the afternoon in Saba. Albert still sleeps. He appears to have improved in comparison with two days ago. His lungs have less infection and fluid and his oxygen flow seems better. Indeed, while I'm with him, gently holding his shoulder, the monitor indicates a leap in the oxygen in his blood. Ketut and I leave feeling optimistic. But it's too early to wake up. The small travel bag I prepared yesterday with a change of clothes, his decades-faithful *Habit Rouge* perfume, a comb, toiletries and even his iPod, comes back with us.

Monday 26 June. Today is Béa's birthday. 57 years old. I'm sorry it has to be like that. I send kind wishes to her in Switzerland from her Papa and me. Our brief stay in Bali was meant to be up tomorrow. We had planned returning briefly to Brisbane, and then to a three-day international film festival in La Foa, a village north of New Caledonia's main airport, before returning to our island home. I work on changing our airline tickets. The girl in Virgin Australia is most accommodating. Late afternoon Ketut and I head to Saba again. The anaesthetist, Dr M, is less encouraging. Albert's oxygen is not so good. What can be still lying infected in his lungs, puzzles the doctor, trying his best to find a solution. Is it fungal? Is it metastasis? We'll continue treatment under coma for another one, two, three days. Oh, my dear Albert.

Ketut and I are down-hearted.

It rains heavily on the way "home". Frightening, the waves of rain that cross the roads and splash up over plastic-covered scooter riders and vehicles alike. There's almost a feeling of possibly being swept away. Ketut explains that the drains, often two metres deep, are choked with plastic, so there's no run-off, no escape for downpours. Poor Bali is drowning 'neath plastic, rubbish in general, buses – ever bigger, carrying ever more visitors, and droves of scooters – the ordinary worker's means of manoeuvring around and faster than all the other hazards. Back at the hotel, I eat, light my candle outside and keep vigil. I don't want to write any more emails. But I've promised to Skype a doctor friend in Australia, a French doctor who knows us, our house, our island, our history. I tell her Dr M's searching for answers. His suggestion that it could be "environmental pneumonia", something of fungal origin, strikes a cord with Dr C. She immediately reminds me we had had a burst water pipe under our kitchen floor before last Christmas. A gaping hole for several days had exposed mud from which emanated a distinctive, mouldy smell. Her medical detective mind began thinking about the possible release of *anaerobic* bacteria, which, she told me, can develop in places without oxygen, such as mud. Bolstered by this possible explanation, I send an email to Dr M via the hospital alarm centre and to his personal address. He kindly replies he'll discuss the idea with his colleagues. I/we can only hope.

Tuesday 27 June. We should have been leaving Ubud and Bali this evening. Our tickets are changed. I pay the hotel till today and book for another week. Fortunately I can keep the same bungalow. Our belongings are here. Albert's hat sits as he left it, turned upwards, his sunglasses resting inside. I feel comfortable here. It's close to the pool. The staff pass by and all take time to say, hello, how are you? The traffic is heavy again in Ubud. Ketut piggybacks me, one might say, on his scooter once again, to his house and car and we take narrow, sinuous back roads, known to locals, to the hospital in Saba. Dr M is not there. Albert lies so still. His heartbeat is low, says the nurse. The oxygen fluctuates. *Oh, la, la.* I watch over him, hold him gently, whisper close to him.

Ketut and I leave disheartened.

He suggests we visit the waterfall at Tegenungan for tea. The quiet road turns into a tourist stop – parking area and souvenir stalls. Nevertheless, we find a table on the terrace overlooking the falls and lush surrounding valley and sip a ginger tea. Two smiling, cute girls in school uniform approach us. Aged 12 and 15, they're doing interviews for their English class. We cooperate, take photos. They cheer the afternoon.

Back along the main road, still driving through the countryside, Mount Agung shows itself on the right-hand side (the driver's side). At just over 3,000 metres above sea level, it's Bali's highest and considered holiest volcano by this Hindu population. Often cloud-covered, Ketut tells me of its erupting the last time in 1963. More than a thousand people died in the flow of boulders and magma. His mother had told him there was no day or night for six months. There was nothing to eat. All the vegetation was covered with ash. It took two years to come back again. Now that ash-enriched soil produces much of Bali's fresh food. Uncanny it is then, that as I write – 24, 25 September 2017 – world news agencies are carrying a story warning that the same volcano has started heating and rumbling. There are reports too that wild animals, including snakes and apes, are descending from the mountain top down to settled areas. According to local belief, this is one sign that an eruption is imminent. Evacuations have begun within the periphery. I pray for Ketut and his family and all the Balinese folk within Agung's reach, that the eruption does not happen, that they will be safe.

Wednesday 28 June. I have a morning rendezvous with the three doctors, Dr M, Dr Y. and the pregnant, internal organs doctor. Albert's heart rate is better. His oxygen has improved. But today is the seventh day in Intensive Care. They've consulted between them and propose a tracheotomy to help his breathing and to enable them to carry out a better detection of what is infecting his lungs – bacterial or viral pneumonia, or metastasis c ... ? It's a chance.

I sign, I pay and above all, I pray. We'll return tomorrow at 9 a.m.

When I say I pay – it's not a tiny affair. The total reads more than 42 million rupiah! – The equivalent of more than $A4,000.

And when will the results be known? I ask. It could take up to seven days, comes the doctors' reply. The swabs need to be sent to Denpasar. But we'll try to use our influence to obtain them more rapidly.

Oh, the anguish. Everything swims in my head. A fat, warm tear rolls down my cheek and drops on to my arm.

Back at the hotel I try to stay calm. Then late afternoon I receive an email from the hospital asking me to sign another clearance for the tracheotomy to go ahead. It's to be performed at nine o'clock tonight. But I already signed this morning. And paid. I don't understand. I query the insistence.

The hospital sends me another paper I have to print off, sign, and re-send. Not easy when one is in a village hotel and has to rely on the kindness and efficiency of the reception staff, as well as, hopefully, the reliability of their office equipment and connections. The form is a complete discharge of responsibility on the part of the hospital. It's headed: High Risk Procedure Consent and reads in English, first, "I understand the need for and benefits of such action as it has described as above for Me, including the risk and complications that may arise." And continues (in Bali English): "I also realized because the medicine is not an exact science, hence the success of the medical act is not a necessity, but very dependent on the permission of God Almighty." "This agreement I made with full awareness and without any coercion".

Oh my God! I feel sick. I reply, signing, but write "Please take note Albert bleeds easily". I ask myself, what if I'm signing Albert into danger and his life away. I feel locked in an inextricable web.

Then it comes to me: yesterday I met an American woman staying with her family at the hotel. We chatted briefly. She was pleasant, open and told me her husband was an Emergency doctor in Los Angeles. She offered that I could talk with him if I wished. Mmm. An emergency doctor in L.A. – he surely needs a holiday, I said to myself, I won't bother him. But now day's end is nearing, it's close to 6 p.m. Terrified by the thought of a tracheotomy on Albert that might go wrong, that I shouldn't have signed so hastily, I dare approach the holidaying doctor. We sit outside on their terrace, just a couple of bungalows away from mine. He kindly explains the process of a tracheotomy. He tells me it should really only take about 20 minutes and that, despite my worries, I should trust the doctors who have proposed and who will perform the operation. Thankyou. I feel a little easier. A couple of hours later the family with three young boys, neatly dressed and beautifully behaved, invites me to sit with them for dinner. The children love to read, and I return with my self-published collection of *Tales & Rhymes from a Paradise Island*, so they can learn a little about my island home, its people and animal life. Chance encounters of kindness are to mark the next few months.

Thursday 29 June. We, Ketut and I, are at the hospital by 10 a.m. Albert is lying quietly. His mouth now more comfortable. The tracheotomy was successful. But, says Dr M, the rapid swab analysis shows the verdict means all the life support is futile and economics have to be considered too. He even broaches the word "euthanasia", saying it's not a practice in Bali. So, once again, I have to summon up courage. He tells me I need to discuss with Béa that tomorrow afternoon will be final. I must come then.

Dr Y is present too. He accompanies me to the guests' area outside the ward. He's sympathetic. Ketut listens too. Suddenly he picks up on the administrative doctor's words "unless a miracle". The glimmer of hope strikes a cord with Ketut. We should go to Denpasar straight away to consult his sister, a spiritual healer. And so with concentration and determination, we drive speedily to the capital on a mission. We wind into what seem small, suburban streets and alleys and lo and behold, in between what appear ordinary houses, stands the entrance to a Hindu temple, ornate statues of painted lions, a gold-headed and tipped snake, open-mouthed, green and gold spotted dragons wearing crowns, plants and parasols, while inside there's a labyrinth of buildings, colourful Indian decorations, steps and altars. Ketut finds Sari and her husband, a holy man. He explains briefly our mission to his sister. We pay her and she leads us along a path to an inner sanctuary. It's dim, tiered, highly decorated with Hindu deities. Clad in white, she climbs on a raised podium, crouches down and begins to chant and pray. She asks for a photo of Albert, which I manage to find and didn't remember I had, in the depths of my wallet. She tells me, through Ketut, that Albert is strong, but there is something the doctors can't see. He may be alright. Maybe not. She instructs us to return to the hospital and perform several rituals, for which she goes away and prepares the ingredients. Bewildered, and a smidgen elated, we return along the highway and turn off to the Saba countryside. I return to Albert's bedside, clutching carefully the little plastic bags filled with peeled garlic cloves and onions in water. I'm desperate and willing to try anything. Oh if it could be a miracle. I follow Sari's instructions, crushing the wet garlic and onion mixture in my hand, rubbing it from the top to bottom of each foot, three times, repeating a phrase I've written down but don't understand enough to have learned so quickly by heart.

My heart thumps. Dear Albert, I'm trying. The nursing staff are not at all disconcerted, nor appear scornful or condescending. It's as if they understand that if their treatment can no longer work, perhaps recourse to a more spiritual way may indeed be possible.

Now I follow with a blessing using a frangipani flower dipped in holy water – descending along his body from the forehead, sternum and pelvic chakra – again, repeated three times. The ritual finishes with our going outside, Ketut and I, his rustling up a 5,000 rupiah note, a 100 rupiah coin – neither common, a little basket of flower offerings, and three lit incense sticks which I then toss, head down like an arrow, into a flowing stream running between the road and the fields.

I pray my own prayers, hoping for a miracle.

THREE

The End – just the beginning

About 4 o'clock in the morning, I wake and decide to light the oil candle outside. I use half a box of matches, but either they break or fizzle out, or the wick's exhausted – whatever, it won't light. I take it as a sign and return, almost resigned, to bed.

Friday 30 June. Ketut and I go early in the morning to Saba. I want to spend the day with Albert until the doctors' promised visit at three in the afternoon. I know it's the last day. I take his white hat, his perfume and put them on the shelf just behind his head. I keep vigil. Tell him how wonderful our life has been together. How he'll stay with me forever.

About 11.45 a.m. I look at my watch. It stopped at 11.17 a.m. Albert's soul has taken wings. The mechanical support is now just that. I go downstairs, numb. Then I return and stay by his side till the doctors arrive about 3.30 p.m. Whether out of compassion, or whether to protect me, Dr Y suggests I should eat something. True, I haven't eaten since my light, early breakfast. I find Ketut. We go, for the first time, into the hospital's guests' restaurant. No other clients are there, but the chef prepares for us a dish suggested for sustenance – *bubur ayam* – a sort of rice porridge with shredded chicken. It takes a while to come; it's warm, tasty, solid. I can't finish it all and I don't have the heart to try. Three quarters of an hour go by before I return upstairs. I walk in to the small ward. A female doctor I've never seen before comes straight to me and says Mr Thoma passed away at 4.15 p.m. From the clock on the wall I see it's now 4.17 p.m. Dear Albert is already white. They've taken his air away. But I know he'd decided to leave on his own terms, in his own time. The official act is a formality.

Almost within minutes, a male nurse approaches the bed with what look like pliers, presumably to disconnect the tubes. Oh the harshness of it all. Oh the detachment required of such a profession. I go downstairs. Ketut is waiting.

We're together now. Alone. I'm alone in the world, except for him. We're like a tiny boat lost at sea. Where do we turn? What do we do? How? When? Who can we talk to? I ask for Dr Y, but it's Friday afternoon, and he's left already. We're ushered in to a closed-off room with a table, a couple of chairs and two small bottles of water. We're informed we have two hours to decide what to do with the body. It all feels so industrial, so inhumane. And then, would you believe, the trim accounts girl arrives with the "final account". This is just too-oo much.

Even though we knew the end was coming, Ketut and I had not discussed what would follow, what we would do, what Albert would wish. It seemed tempting fate to broach the subject. And now, while having to face reality in haste, we also have another pressing rendezvous. Let's say one guardian angel was with us in thought, and was winging his way to us, literally. I had kept my family and Albert's informed from the first moment he was admitted to hospital. This morning, my dear brother who lives in Brisbane, and his wife, conferred with one another then sent me a message: Would I like Jeremy to join me? My reply was unequivocally "Yes", to which, within minutes, he had found a ticket via Internet and within hours was on a plane for the near six-hour flight to Denpasar. Oh what a comforting surprise, what a God-send, and throughout the next week, what incredible support in every way, not just for me, but also empathetic company for Ketut. Ubud-born and bred, Ketut has become more and more a friend, an advisor, although of course I pay him daily as a driver. Jeremy is an angel at any time – clear-headed, endowed with common sense and the ability to cut through hazy, cluttered ideas -- it's no wonder he's one of the directors of the university where he works, even though in his self-deprecating way, he describes his job as filling in where others don't wish to go.

Time is ticking over fast in every sense. Day is drawing to a close. We have two hours to go somewhere with our dear Albert – but physically, really, what can we do? A big body, 1 metre 83 cm, around 105 kg. My being hit over the head already with hospital bills, and refusal by our travel and health insurance to come to our rescue, means there is no way of even considering repatriating back to New Caledonia, plus it's gone 9 p.m. Friday night there, where all offices would be long shut.

Ketut wisely suggests that as Albert so dearly wanted to come to Bali, he might like to embrace their Hindu way and that we offer him a traditional cremation funeral. At the back of my mind the word "cremation" had also been hovering. Albert and I had talked briefly of that a year or two ago. He'd told me that would be his preference. We had even imagined the logistics from our island home. But when we looked into costs of arranging it all in the capital, Noumea, it was too exorbitant and we said, forget it; then began setting money aside, assiduously, for the day it might/would come. Never dreaming for one second that it would strike far from home, in a foreign country, a foreign culture. That conscientiousness on our part turned out to be a nasty slap in the face later on.

Meanwhile, here we are – alone, bereft, bewildered, left to fend for ourselves.

The accounts girl tells us we can take Albert's body to one of two morgues – in Denpasar or in a country hospital in Gianyar, the administrative centre of Ubud region, a pleasant, non-tourist town we've visited a couple of times to meet the family that we've dealt with to make fine, cotton shirts for Albert to paint. I dislike the idea of going anywhere near the Bali capital, Denpasar. It would be impersonal, noisy, crowded. We say we'll opt for Gianyar, about 15 km from the hospital and 13 km from Ubud. She then explains quite crudely that the morgue is not refrigerated, that the bodies are treated with formalin. We shrug our shoulders. That's what we'll have to accept.

So now what? Every minute is ticking by. It's getting dark. We're told an ambulance will take Albert's body to Gianyar. We have to go down to the parking lot in the basement at the back of the building. Will I ride in the ambulance or will I ride behind with Ketut? I opt for the latter. I feel we can keep a watch on Albert that way. The ambulance driver is careful, respectful. We pull out on to the road and head north, slowly, through the dark, unlit countryside, silhouettes of trees here and there, almost no traffic. It's surreal. It takes perhaps 25 minutes to reach town. We turn into narrow streets then into a dark alleyway squeezed between low buildings. There seem to be people around. It's dark. Several cars line up, we sit in line waiting, then stop beside a building. The driver goes to find the person in charge. He comes back accompanied by a youngish man who turns out to be the embalmer. I've never met an embalmer before, nor ever even considered such a trade. Now I can't quite believe that a young, fresh-looking person would have such a job. He opens the double door and there, in the dim light, we distinguish a row of bodies on waist-high biers – eight or ten, all feet facing the wall. To the right is a concrete slab, working area. Not without difficulty, they remove Albert's body from the ambulance and place it on the bare concrete. Then the driver withdraws the stretcher, strips off the white covering cloth, folds it under his arm and there leaves my dear man totally denuded. I am aghast. What can I cover him with? How can I dignify the moment? I'm wearing a long, ruby red, silk scarf. Can I cover Albert with this? But it's neither wide enough, nor long enough. Oh the indignity, the severity, the bareness of death. I look around for Ketut, but can't find him. Then I'm called to follow the ambulance driver. A man of slight build, a kind face, and I need to pay him. The bill is the equivalent of $A40 – a small sum, I consider, for his work and care. I imagine his going home to his family after such a job. It seems a gulf to cross.

I return inside the morgue. The embalmer is there wearing a white, medical face mask and holding a syringe. Ketut has reappeared. It turns out he was away for what seemed a long time, 15 to 20 minutes. He had gone to find a stall to buy several lengths of sarong material, in brown tones, similar to coverings on the other bodies. How sympathetic and considerate of him. I am relieved and deeply grateful. He and the embalmer cover Albert. We take our leave.

We feel denuded ourselves. Numb. Lost for words. Lost for Albert. A gaping unknown lies before us. At the same time, we're shaken into consulting our watches and being mindful that every minute now is important. It's already after 9 o'clock. Here we are, in mid south-east Bali, in the opposite direction to the International Ngurah Rai airport on the other side of Denpasar, where we are scheduled to meet Jeremy arriving from Brisbane in just over an hour. Thankfully Ketut has petrol in the car. He sets off towards Denpasar, back past the hospital then along the highway leading in to the capital.

Unbelievably, halfway along the faster yet sombre autoroute, we're signalled to pull onto the side of the road. Some one hundred policemen, machine-guns slung over their shoulders, line all sides of the several lanes road, in each direction. There's no way of whisking through. Ketut realises it's a once-a-year operation, checking papers, but in particular searching for drugs. Three police surround the car. They look at Ketut's papers. Then open the boot. There's little in it, but their rustling around finds a bottle of whisky. They make a few remarks, but don't linger. Ketut tells me afterwards, a visitor had left it for him months ago, and he had never taken it out of the car. We continue on our way. It's fairly quiet when we arrive at the airport. The flight from Brisbane hasn't yet arrived. We realise we haven't eaten anything since our rice porridge mid-afternoon. Now it's after 10 p.m. We opt for a creamy vegetable curry, airport-canteen style. It settles us a bit. Then we look for Jeremy and have no trouble finding him. But we have to tell him our sad news – Albert has already slipped away. Just 13 days earlier, we had shared a steak dinner and a glass or two of red together with Jeremy and family in Brisbane on our way to Bali. Nothing had led us to suspect it would be the last family gathering. The return to Ubud, via a different road, is in a sort of vacuum. It's around midnight. Ubud streets are quiet. We're all sledge-hammered.

FOUR

Waiting for an auspicious day

Saturday 1 July. It's comforting having the company of my youngest brother. We've arranged with Ketut to have the morning to ourselves, with a rendezvous planned for this afternoon. I don't know how I'm going to prepare Jeremy for our visit to Albert in the morgue. I tell Ketut I'd like to take a bouquet. He gathers various tropical flowers from the hotel garden, with a small, fuchsia rose (just as we have at home), in the centre. His wrapping – one big taro leaf.

Leading off from the frequented, touristy Monkey Forest Road where we're staying, Jeremy and I find a quiet, open-air restaurant on the edge of a vivid green rice field for lunch – it's solace. A *Bintang,* the renowned, pale, Indonesian lager, is in order. Jeremy orders satay and I fried rice, but my dish goes down with difficulty. How can I eat? I jumble English and French when I try to describe how I feel.

I have "bees" in my tummy, I tell Jeremy, later remembering that in English we say we have "butterflies in the stomach" to explain the nervous sensation that overwhelms me. It's a sensation I still have three months later, ten months later; a sensation verging on nausea; an empty, anguish that won't go away. I write to a friend in Australia: "Life is difficult, despite lovely little kindnesses. I still feel as if I've been gouged out from my neck to the pit of my stomach – it's physically painful. The sea is a help, the good weather too."

Mid-afternoon. We three head off to Gianyar, 13 km drive from Ubud. Despite being the administrative capital for the district that includes Ubud, and its renown for the traditional Balinese *batik* and *ikat* textile factories, as well as garment-producing families, it's decidedly un-touristy and gives off a refreshing authenticity for a medium-sized town going about its own business. We park along a main, tree-lined boulevard and walk a narrow back street to the morgue. There's a calm atmosphere. It all looks so different from the "sinister" feel of last night. Putu, the young embalmer lets us in. We're the only visitors. There, third along, so much bigger than the rest of the occupants, lies Albert. I lay our bouquet on his midriff, and hug his head covered in the sarongs that Ketut bought last night. Jeremy is brave. He takes a look at dear Albert – the elder one he always considered a brother, and whom Albert always called "Arthur", with a cheery, mutual slap on the back.

Words seem superfluous. We wander outside. Shaken. Ketut smokes cigarette after cigarette.

Now we've settled on cremation, we have to start with the practicalities. Seeing we're here in Gianyar, we decide to buy the clothes we'll need. We drive to the main street. We park in a secure parking area then wander through market stall after market stall. It's flagrant where so many clothes in western outlets come from. Stand after stand of shorts, shirts, tee-shirts, sandals, and then on to more interesting produce stalls; local women buying vegetables, chickens, fruit, flowers and spices. Then we come to a covered building housing food and textiles – little businesses tucked in, packed in, a bit like the Russian market in Phnom Penh – material from floor to ceiling and just enough room for the salesperson, one or two family members and a customer or two.

Jeremy and I need sarongs and ceremonial sashes for our waists, I need a long-sleeved fitting top, a *kebaya*, preferably white, and Jeremy an *udeng* – men's head-dress somewhat like a turban. The colours are up to us. I choose a daffodil yellow sarong and matching sash to wear over a fitting blouse that feels good to slip into. Jeremy chooses a white wrap to wear over a heavy cotton, pale grey sarong, a white *udeng w*ith a shot of silver, and a black sash. We buy extra beautiful sarongs for the family in Queensland. Ketut bargains down the price a bit, but the saleslady and her husband are delighted with their important sale.

This is the beginning of our expenses. From now on they climb and climb. Traditional Balinese-Hindu cremations are of three rankings: for the poor, medium range, or for the rich with a multi-storeyed canopied bier. Ketut suggests the most appropriate would be medium range. We would have the funeral services of a holy man and temple, transport for the body from the morgue many kilometres away to the cremation area, then the actual ceremony with offerings, priests and fire. Tomorrow we will go to the country south-west of Ubud to meet a holy man and decide on what day the ceremony will take place. From what he gathers, Ketut believes Monday or Tuesday will be acceptable. It's now Saturday. We're booked to leave Bali on Friday. It's tight. It turns out differently.

Back at the hotel, my small iPad is already awash with condolence emails. I've written to close family and two or three friends, but I'm astonished at the haste and the amount of messages generated, it seems, by my having informed, out of politeness, one couple too many. I'm taken aback at hearing already from people we almost never see or never hear from, or with whom we have little in common. Our own priest back home on the island tells me there's no stopping the word spreading like wildfire.

Sunday 2 July. This morning we meet Made, a family friend and neighbour of Ketut. He apparently knows the temple and its holy men. The two drive us through the country to a temple complex where we're to meet a "holy man". His position commands respect, meaning we need to dress correctly with full-length sarongs, take off our shoes and sit cross-legged on tatami-style mats covering a raised podium. The exercise is horribly painful for Jeremy who has hip problems, but he does his best. A smiling, portly gentleman, the holy man, dressed in white, sports huge rings on both hands and obvious gold deposits in his teeth. We're not at all sure if we're being taken for a ride by "Mr Goldfinger", as Jeremy dubs him later, having also noticed a sparkling new, Japanese-brand motor-bike in the adjacent courtyard. He asks us official questions, with go-between help from Made. While they cover the usual name, address queries, there comes one question that isn't at all common to our occidental line of inquiry: where was Albert placed in his family – first-born or …? He was fourth, I reply. So his name is Ketut! Yes, every fourth-born child in

Hindu Bali tradition is named Ketut (meaning "little banana"). There's a soft twitter amongst us; Ketut our friend and driver is obviously so named, and Jeremy too is fourth-born, so he's also Ketut. It's a small, feel-good sign of similarity and belonging.

But now comes the question and the main reason for our coming: **when** will the cremation be? We've been preparing ourselves for tomorrow, Monday, or the next day. Ketut has told us the day has to be auspicious. If not, the holy man will not, cannot, give his go-ahead and it could be that there would be no cremation for up to three months. Oh no. The suspense. Our host hoists out before him a poster-sized calendar with roman numerals, Sanskrit signs and images.

We can distinguish numbers in numerical order that stand out, big and bold. The holy man starts to run his finger down the left-hand column, the numbers corresponding with our dates: 2, 3 (tomorrow) – no, 4 (Tuesday) – no, 6 – Thursday, he stops. Jeremy and I exchange glances. Thursday is getting close to our departure; it'll be cutting things finely. Then the holy man's finger slides back – 5, Wednesday. There'll be a number of cremations that day. It's a good day. Your cremation will be number six of six. They'll be held in pairs. You need to be here around 11 in the morning to pay the full complement of the fifty million rupiah (approaching A$5000). The ceremony will start at 1 p.m. For the moment you can pay the deposit. Since last night we've rustled up the 10 percent deposit and count it out nervously, then await the receipt. While we can read the figures, there's nothing else we can understand on the pink slip that resembles any corner store docket. We're not at ease. But what can we do? We can only continue. We've still a long way to go, yet it feels as if we've broached so much already.

After wandering around the temple buildings and grounds, we drive a short kilometre through rice-fields to the actual cremation site. There are ceremonies in progress, and walking amidst the attendees towards the altars gives us an idea what we can expect on Wednesday. The whole dominates an impressive, swift-flowing river. Made and Ketut had an excellent idea bringing us here now. Wednesday might be just one blur. The area is called Cekomaria (pronounced Chiko-maria). Ketut remembers by roguishly linking it to the sound of *chikungunya*. We don't forget it either. Indeed, we will never forget it. While there's a big, can't-be-missed "Krematorium" sign on the road-side, Cekomaria is not at all a tourist venue and is difficult to find on any map and absent from travellers' infor-mation. We are being launched into authenticity. How strange. How privileged, in a sense, to be swept up in Balinese-Hindu ritual. Come Wednesday, not once are we made to feel like outsiders. The only questioning I encounter comes late that afternoon while sitting around waiting for the actual cremation fire to end, one puzzled man asks why we have chosen the Hindu way.

Back to Sunday. It's been a dense morning. We can't leave Albert alone in Gianyar. We return again. This time late in the afternoon. I take a single rose from the hotel garden. Ketut kindly buys a candle and a tiny basket of flower offerings. All's quiet around the morgue. It's Sunday. We're worried it might be closed. But no. We push the door and let ourselves in. The building is nothing more than a simple shed. It's all surreal, but at the same time it's all so real and unpretentious. We are close.

In the quiet of late afternoon we three stroll the length of Gianyar's avenue of *Pama* trees – tall, ribbon-like leaved trees that resemble giant folded parasols and said to be an aid in absorbing carbon dioxide. Our walk takes us to a peaceful, tidy garden with coloured water fountains, music, lights – happy children and families picnicking – a gentle glimpse of normality.

Monday 3 July. Ring, ring. Ring, ring. Our silent hotel room is startled by the phone ringing unexpectedly. The voice at the other end is even more unexpected. More surrealism. "Frau Thoma?" What? Yes. I don't speak German, but I understand that much.

And so begins our nightmare with the Honorary German Consulate, based in Sanur, a good hour's drive south from Ubud. And what do they have to do with us? Well it turns out Albert, while born in Switzerland, was the son of immigrants – his father, of German origin, settled in the land of the red and white square flag when he was about five. His mother's family came from Modena, Italy, home of Pavarotti and balsamic vinegar. They too moved to the little country just north looking for work, way back when Nelda (Albert's mother) was three. Ever since, the family had considered themselves Swiss. Deep in their hearts, they came from the village where Albert and his siblings were born in the German-speaking part of the country. They went to school and church there, they worked there and paid their taxes, they spoke unwritten Swiss German at home and 'haute deutsch', High German or official German, at school. But Switzerland doesn't tolerate immigrants easily. You can't just slip across the border, become a refugee, hope to stay and become a national. No. Even if you are born on Swiss soil, you are not entitled to its nationality, unless your parents were born there too. So how do you become Swiss, if you're born there, but are not of there? You have to buy your citizenship. And it doesn't come cheaply. Years ago it was around A$1000 a head. Buying citizenship entitles its holder to vote and to being eligible for the compulsory national service so respected in the ostensibly neutral country. One of Albert's brothers bought the nationality for himself, his English wife and his four sons. Albert and his other brother, both a-political, never did. The result meant their passports took their father's nationality.

So here we are. In Ubud, Bali. About to embark on a traditional Hindu-Balinese cremation, and we have the honorary German consulate summoning me to their office. How on earth …?

Jeremy and I mutter.

It turns out the hospital has been diligent. The paper documenting Albert's death, includes passport, specifying German, for his European passport. The hospital has notified the consulate that a German national has died in its care. I should present myself there straight away. Ketut comes to our rescue once again. This is not how we had planned our Monday. We have money problems to attend to. We need to concentrate on plans for Wednesday. But no. Here we are, heading to Sanur. Mid-morning, beginning of the week. Road-users hustle and bustle, traffic fills the roads leading to Sanur. Once there, it's not easy to find the famous honorary consulate. It turns out to be indicated by a tiny sign, leading down a luxuriant alley, within arm's length of sweeping Sanur beach. Some German consulate staff have a cushy job, we think to ourselves. It might sound swanky having a consulate in Bali, but it turns out to be a rather neglected outpost, even the lockers to place bags in before entering the office, are falling apart, the lock fixture comes off in our hands. Inside, it's Kafkaesque. I'm told I have to have a paper signed by the registry office and by the Honorary Consul. He's absent until Monday. We're scheduled to leave the Friday before. No-one has authority to sign for him. There's a distinct ring of the 1950s. There's even a typewriter! They cannot give us any helpful addresses. We're up against a blank wall. We start to see red and get out of there, having got nowhere.

We three decide to take a look at the well-known beach, as we're parked on the edge. It's wide, wind-swept, uncrowded. But we don't pick up good vibes. We feel better heading back to Ubud. Our morning "misadventure" is just the start of hurdles to overcome, one by one, before Wednesday. We need to start withdrawing millions of rupiahs from the bank, but we try three establishments before finding one that will give us even a quarter of the sum we need. The others had limits of a tenth of what we need. We would have to return for five or ten days, but our cut off point is tomorrow night. Not only is the cash payment needed for the cremation hanging over our heads, but the hospital now starts hassling me for payment. The same night they send me an email threatening to come to the hotel, some 40 minutes drive away, and take my passport as collateral. Oh my God. This is plunging in mire. My bank too has a limit on daily withdrawals. We connect by Skype with its, thankfully, pleasant understanding staff and ask for their intervention. In the nether world of international banking it turns out transfers can take more than two weeks before reaching their destination, causing unwarranted anguish, veering into distrust and unpleasantness.

Tuesday 4 July. We decide to go early to Albert today. I take a twin rose that has flowered this morning. Putu, the moustached, kind-faced young man who embalmed Albert, greets and accompanies us. After our quiet time with Albert, we head to the administration office. I pay the equivalent of $5.00 a night for five nights and a little extra for cooling. Derisory costs bordering on pathos, if the situation wasn't all so dramatic, so unreal.

Lots of people are around today in the street behind – the poor lining up for poor people's treatment, as Ketut explains. We three return to the market where we bought our ceremonial clothes for more gifts, then decide on an early lunch so Jeremy can try Gianyar's and Bali's famous *Babi Guling* – spit-roasted suckling pig – generous, delicious, the dish is traditionally served with a big chunk of crackling, tender meat perfumed with herb and spice stuffing, black pudding – pork blood sausage, rice, mixed vegetables and a clear soup. Unaccustomed as we are to eating a hearty plate mid-morning, it turns out be an excellent idea, sustaining us well into the early evening. The rest of the day we spend between the banks, rustling up what cash we can in our travel folders, finding money we'd put aside for later in the trip, and being called back to the hospital by the unrelenting accounts girls. And I'd thought last Friday was the very last time I'd ever set foot in that institution again. Affronted at being so harassed by the matter I frankly care least about, I dare inquire as to who owns this private hospital so intent on collecting its enormous charges. A Balinese gynaecologist, comes the reply; he owns four private hospitals on the island. A lucrative profession indeed.

FIVE

... and on the 5th day

There are certain days in your life when every trivial detail stands out in your memory as if stamped in wax. Graham Greene, *Death in Geneva*

Wednesday 5 July. The above line slotted into a novel I wrote in the early nineties. Did it presage my own experience on 5 July 2017? Coincidence or not, I have no notes concerning that day, yet every detail reverberates in my mind's eye.

The solemn day dawns a day one would never wish to face; its having done so, one could only wish it would be over in a flash. Neither is true.

The nightmare of the past five days has reached its culmination. We can only continue. Once again, dear God, thank you for sending Jeremy. We know what we have to do. We've prepared our clothes; we've prepared the 90 per cent payment we still owe the holy man, his temple and the *krematorium*, scouring every last pocket for dollars to change, complementing the withdrawals the bank has allowed us at such short notice; I pluck the one small fuchsia rose in bloom at the edge of the garden; I hold its head with care for the next few hours until I can place it next to Albert.

We dress in our newly acquired ceremonial attire. A sarong is my daily wardrobe at home on our island, yet I'm unaccustomed to tying one Balinese-style. A discreet, older hotel employee stops by and checks the knots, then drapes the daffodil yellow, heavy cotton length as it should be. He checks Jeremy's attire too. We're to go to the *krematorium* in the country in two cars. Made has borrowed a spanking new, white, four-wheel drive. Jeremy and I will go with him. Ketut will follow with his wife and parents-in-law who've asked to accompany us. During the day their unspoken, strong support turns out to be manifest.

It's mid-week. Other people are going about their regular lives. It's 10 a.m. We set off down the heart road of Ubud, turn right and there's not a car in front of us. We continue turning out of town, through the nearby villages and countryside, and still, the way opens up in front of us. There's not a vehicle in front. Nothing is impeding us. Nothing is slowing us. It's as if we have a presidential opening without the clamour. Is an angel guiding us?

We arrive unflustered at the temple for our rendezvous with the holy man – chief cashier. We're beckoned to mount the podium and to hand over our rupiahs in their millions. This time we receive an official receipt entitled in wording we can read. "*Ouf*", we sigh, now we have the official paper demanded by the German honorary consulate. One more hurdle overcome, we reckon quietly.

We slip down from the podium, Jeremy takes some photos – all seven of us, ritually attired, colourful. We're shown temple work - sheets of Sanskrit verses written on cloth, then wander through several buildings to a neat garden where in the shade of an elaborate, gold-leaf decorated, raised kiosk, four men practise traditional gamelan music – not for tourists, its authenticity sets the tone for the rites about to begin.

Morning is coming to a close. We drive through green rice fields to the *krematorium*, parking the cars in a wide, tree-surrounded, open space in a dip, several minutes walk from the ceremonial area. Food vendors line the river with various little stalls of hot and cold food and drinks. Given the number of cremations today, the number of mourners, family and friends, understandably counts in the hundreds. They stand around in the sun, in the shade, sit on balustrades near the river, or on stools in the food stalls. All beautifully and suitably dressed, the men kepi-topped, the women colourful, sometimes lacy, their stance dignified from so many years of carrying wares on their head. They chat, wait patiently. No-one cries.

Ketut suggests we should eat. Jeremy and I are neither hungry nor really interested, but our friend knows best. We have five hours of ceremony ahead of us. We'll need some sustenance. It turns out he's more than right. So we follow suit, opting for a bowl of chicken balls, vegetables and hard-boiled egg in a steaming, but not too spicy broth. It's comforting, once again highlighting Balinese wisdom of the right food for the right moment.

One o'clock is approaching. Streams of people are leaving, signalling the end of the ceremonies before ours. Two white ambulance/hearses draw up, inching their way forward. We follow. There's no coffin. Just the bier and Albert's body draped as it was in the morgue. Whoever oversaw the transfer from Gianyar had the heart and thoughtfulness to leave the two roses I'd taken yesterday on top. Ketut tips the driver who's come a long way from the capital. Albert is heavy and imposing. All of a sudden there's a flurry of helpers to lift him out and up the steps to the mortuary area, laying him on a woven mat covering a waist-high, four-poster bier, like a king-size four-poster bed, the posts and surrounds wrapped in Balinese black and white large checked ceremonial cloth, the backdrop too, of the same black and white material on which is hung an etching in delicate grey and white. In front, at the top of the steps, are platters covered with banana leaf, bananas, eggs, cooked rice, offering baskets of miniature flowers, and incense sticks. As well as a big bucket of water.

But first, it's prayer time. We sit cross-legged on the concrete ground. A holy man has colourful baskets in front of him, a basket of petals and a small bell. Our small coterie has swelled to some 25 or 30 people joined in prayer, taking a pinch of flowers between our fingers, raising our hands and following with appropriate gestures.

We stand and move to the bier, for now begins the cleansing and purification, both literal and symbolic. Thoughtful as ever, Ketut and his wife have brought soap and towel, a comb, metres and metres of white cloth for the shroud. He's even slipped in Albert's *Habit Rouge* after-shave I'd given him when we left the hospital and which he was keeping in his car door pocket. The body is to be unwrapped and washed publicly in the warm, open air. I have the feeling there are at least ten helpers gathered on all sides. But before, one young, gentle holy man taps me on the shoulder, hands me a square of heavy cloth about the size of a lady's handkerchief. I'm Albert's wife. I'm to slip the cloth under the other coverings and slide it up to his private parts. This I'm to hold in place, while the lathering and washing begins in earnest. The yellow soap froths and swirls in the sloshing. After the drying, I'm handed an egg. This I'm to roll down the length of Albert from the top of his head to his feet then smash it on the ground. The purification continues. The holy man hands me a brownish knob of what seems like resin. This I'm to rub on any wounds. As Albert had undergone the last ditch tracheotomy, he still has the stitches; my action on the hollow of his neck will heal, seal the wound, purify his departure from this world. My partner of 42 years always wore white – it was his signature. I've brought his white long pants and favourite shirt with blue totem painted down one side. I can't figure out how we can dress him. My guides settle that. They begin wrapping his body in the long white shroud, lay Albert's shirt on his chest and arms, then finish off the wrapping, laying cloth squares on top inscribed in handwritten Sanskrit, the towel folded at the head holding a small basket of flowers, while two garlands of small, vivid orange chrysanthemums are lain cross-wise on top. Calm and peace emanate.

As if from nowhere, appear tiny plaited baskets after tiny plaited baskets of flowers and grasses all along one side of the woven mat where Albert's beautifully wrapped body lies. At the head, next to my roses, stands an ornate, fan-shaped bouquet of yellow and white frangipani tied with a green ribbon. We're beginning to see that the whole procedure is indeed a costly affair. So many people, so much organisation, so much attention to detail. Not to mention the time, the devotion, the pervading aura in which we are enmeshed. No-one is a spectator. Everyone participates.

Now it's time to celebrate. We're swept into a snake dance, one behind the other, all the while invited to nibble on small skewers of a tasty, peppery, possibly chicken sausage. Sustenance for the next world. Now follow more prayers on a higher level. We stand in front of an altar behind which preside two regally crowned priests; bare shoulders and arms, their swarthy bodies swaddled tightly in heavy, woven, grey-green cloth, long strings of black and white seed necklaces, both moustached, the older one a 10-centimetre silver goatee beard, and on both faces an intense, piercing look denotes the severity of the approaching cremation. The altar itself is laden with woven pandanus platters of more little basket offerings, green and yellow coconuts, incense sticks, oil and candles on ornate raised stands and an intriguing beaten bronze urn containing I know not what – perhaps holy water? Small bells and frangipani complete the array of utensils and decorations for the ensuing chants and prayers.

The hours are indeed accumulating. It's time now to move the body. Much shuffling ensues, while as many men as possible and some women help lift the bier. Jeremy too is caught in the heavy duty. I'm worried he might trip, but he gallantly takes his part alongside Ketut and the others. The rest of us are linked holding a long, thick cord as we almost slide down the slope some 30 or 40 metres to the actual funeral pyre. The fires for the last two cremations are about to be lit. The ceremony is public again; there's chanting and snake dancing. Someone hands me a small earthenware pot with a lighted candle. When we come to a stop, I place this at the foot beneath Albert's corpse. Other participants have already placed flowers and candles on top, and one lady tweaks me, inquiring "he likes to smoke?" – She's poked two slim white cigarettes on top as her contribution.

The signal comes to start the fire. There's no way I can stay. Most of the other women don't stay either. Some of the men remain a while. We climb the rise and head to a sitting area in the open. We're in for a long wait – an hour? An hour and a half? Naturally a particular smoky smell wafts up on the whoosh of the fire. The harsh reality is still so surreal. Is this how it feels to be a stunned mullet? To be in a no world, yet in an ordinary world where people sit around, chat a bit, drinking warm, sweet, creamy coffee.

I have time to wander to the next altar. This time a banquet of sweets, desserts for the journey, is laid out; tiny, banana leaf-lined baskets displaying pink and white, yellow and green delicacies, of coconut and cane sugar, nuts and skewers, small triangular banana leaf bundles wrapped in pink ribbon and a tall floral decoration with the ticket "Albert, Ubud". Behind, stands the holy man from the washing ceremony, waiting to pray and ring bells at the arrival of the ashes.

All quietens as the impetus of the incineration slows down. The men in the families are summoned to collect the ashes and accompany them to the festive, dessert altar. Some of the ashes have been put in a bright yellow coconut. Some are there in the open, on round, silver platters. We're handed a pestle and invited to participate, to take turns in grinding some of the incineration remains! Where in the world, at least in the western world, do you grind your loved one's bones to a finer ash? It's a strange, haunting sensation. A fleeting sensation I quickly opt not to continue. Ketut has brought three little, plastic-lined, rattan boxes in which to put separate lots of ash, as we'd arranged with him. One for Béatrice, Albert's daughter in Switzerland; one for me to carry back to Isle of Pines, and one for me to post to myself, in case the box in my carry-on bag is seized by customs, through which I'll need to pass at least three times: out of Indonesia, in to and then out of Australia, and on arrival in New Caledonia. I have no idea how my declaration will be received.

The thanksgiving prayers for a "sweet" soul journey begin. The crowd has thinned now. We're almost on our own. Indeed, after these, we think are final prayers, we're ushered to another balcony overlooking the river. More bells, more flowers and prayers, led by another holy man. He indicates that we're to pick up the yellow coconut, some platters and flowers. He then takes his leave. Now we are just the seven of us, as we started out this morning.

Day is drawing to a close. It's nearly six o'clock. We head down some decidedly steep steps to the river's edge. The other side of the swiftly flowing waterway is lined with large, dark trees. In an opening between them, silhouettes of grand Bali kites glide in the pink-tinged sky. Adieu dear Albert, as we cast his ashes into the river that will carry them far along to the Bali Sea – to the sea that became his element more than 50 years earlier, the sea he loved and loved to share as a scuba-diver and underwater guide.

We climb the steps and wander through the crematorium grounds along the river bank – silent, shaken, bewildered, lost. Dusk has descended. We three women wait on the roadside while the men go to get the two cars. We wait and we wait. We don't say much, but we're perplexed. Ketut's mother-in-law is cold. I rub her arms and try to say they're coming. Then Ketut appears. By now it's night. It's dark. There's no light in the parking area below. The only lights are from the odd, passing vehicle. What's up? Ketut's car has not the slightest bit of life in it! It won't start. It's given up the ghost. It's in total harmony with the day, the end. The car that has driven me hundreds of kilometres over the past two and a half weeks has also died.

Jumper starts are of no avail; phone calls, waiting in solidarity in the dark, finally more than two hours later, a Japanese car specialist arrives from Gianyar. He's smartly thought to bring a new battery. The faithful vehicle spurts to life again. We all head "home" to Ubud, wrung out. Life will never be the same again – for any of us.

Fresh out of television - Christmas 1976.

40 years later - December 2016.

Gadji, Isle of Pines 1982.

Noumea, July 2016, with his grand-daughter, Kasmira, named after the coral reef fish, *Lutjanus Kasmira*, the scientific name for the pretty blue-stripe snapper.

In recent years we travelled during the Southern Hemisphere 'cool season'. Vallodolid in the Yucatan, Mexico, 2007 - after exploring Mayan ruins and the natural cenotes caves.

Jules, Albert's grandson, Bali, 2010.

Albert, with daughter Béa, in her garden, Vevey, Switzerland, 2011.

B.B. (Brigitte Bardot) and Albert were both born in 1934.
Here with old friend, Jean-Claude, Hong Kong, 2011.

With long-time friends in old Montreux village, Switzerland, 2013.

Albert in his studio, 2014 (photo courtesy J.K. Deret).

Albert never drove a car.

SIX

White sand, warm sun, French food...

*If you really want to get away from it all,
go to where there's white sand, warm sun, French food, the Isle of Pines.*

One other day stands indelible in my memory, etched "as if stamped in wax", all so clear. It's the day I met Albert in March 1975. The circle is now complete.

Working in broadcasting in Australia, I used to take leave to return to my family in New Zealand. For once, I decided I'd take a break to the islands. I'd thought of Fiji, but when I went to book on a Saturday in mid-city Sydney, the travel agent fobbed me off! "Come back Monday", she said. I went home to the beautiful house I rented in the woods verging on Wahroonga reserve, spread out *The Saturday Australian*, and chanced upon an article about a hotel in Noumea, the *Chateau Royal*. At the end of the story read three lines:

If you really want to get away from it all, Go to where there's white sand, warm sun, French food, the Isle of Pines.

That was it. No Fiji. I'd settle for the temptation that journalist Geraldine Pascal had tacked on to her story. I'd never heard of Isle of Pines, but wasn't fazed. I'd just turned 29. I was a news and current affairs journalist, had been in Australia seven years, interviewing artists, tradesmen, union representatives, politicians including Prime Ministers, I'd thrilled at the adventure of driving from Perth to Sydney in five days in my Fiat *850 coupé*. I loved challenges. Little scared me. A break on a French Pacific island would suit me well. Within a few days I was on my way.

Overnight in Noumea, I switched on the radio – it was in French, it was exotic. The next afternoon, at Magenta domestic airport, my fellow passengers flouted "JUST MARRIED". Whoops, where was I going?

Not to mind. I'm going for the trilogy of white sand, warm sun, French food, to talk to no-one, mind my own business, escape from the hurly-burly of politics and everyday news, as well as distance myself from a triangular attachment I had with a colleague-cameraman, against my better judgement.

I remember little of the flight to Isle of Pines, or arrival at its unassuming airport, or the red dust road from the plateau, but sublime was the sweeping crescent of white sand once we reached Kuto. Stunning. Geraldine Pascal wasn't wrong. To top if off, the island's only hotel straddled an isthmus linking that amazing bay to another, equally poetic. My thatched bungalow, no. 33, overlooked Kanumera Bay, facing the light south-east breezes. It was late afternoon. Being the only hotel, meant it offered the only place to eat and drink. So what better to do than wander along the water's edge to the hotel terrace fronting a giant coral rock?

A tall, slender, sun-tanned man approached me: Would I like a drink? I can still see him: longish hair, almost none on top, powder-blue eyes, a long string of shells, lei-like, around his neck, an orange and white *paréo/* sarong knotted around his hips. The stuff of a third rate movie. I fell right in. I, who'd come to do nothing, talk to no-one.

My planned five-day stay turned to ten, I returned to Sydney, announced I was going to resign my good, indeed wonderful, job as an A-grade journalist, and live on an island. I hardly knew the person who would be my companion, I didn't speak the language and I would have little money! It might last six months, I thought. My father had often said: "Never regret anything". His advice echoed in my head. If I go, I could always return to the high-flying life in television or radio. If I don't go, I'll probably always reprimand myself: what if …? So I listened to my father. I was obliged to give three months' notice and wait two more months for a visa. What was a female, political journalist doing going to live on a French outpost in the Pacific? The stern warning came when I picked up my visa from the French consulate in Sydney: "You can have this if you do nothing to offend the French government!" That was it. My mouth and pen were stymied from the beginning. Love and adventure came at a price – the price of compromise.

I had been on the island only two months, when the Whitlam government running Australia was sacked. Channel Ten needed more journalists. They called me, on the island's only phone at the post office. Albert and I were building our house. The first words I'd learned in French were, "Pass me the hammer and the nails". But perhaps the heady swirl of tempestuous politics and journalism was really my life. Albert came with me to Noumea. We bought two dresses and a pair of high heels (I'd given everything sophisticated away). I returned to Sydney. One month away convinced me that my life was indeed on the island with a man 12 years older, a man whose first language was Swiss-German, second German, third French, fourth a smattering of English. A man whose passion, scuba-diving, had lured him away from his graphic-designer life in Switzerland, to join in setting up a small underwater business in the French South Pacific. A man with whom I felt comfortable, for whom I surrendered my career in exchange for a life along a path less travelled. A path we forged and shared for the next 42 years.

We often said in recent times, "How quickly it's gone".

"When you're courting a nice girl," Einstein reportedly declared, *"an hour seems like a second. When you sit on a red-hot cinder a second seems like an hour. That's relativity".*

Our 42 years flashed by. I cannot believe I'm in my early seventies. Albert's stance, curiosity, energy and enthusiasm for life belied his 83 summers.

SEVEN

A rose

Life's what happens
When you're making other plans.
John Lennon

Here I am, still in the exotic isle of Bali, my youngest brother for stalwart company and all that remain of Albert - three small boxes of ashes.

The day following the cremation awakens a beautiful day. The half-hidden rose bush that had provided me with single-bloom stems to offer Albert the past five days, blooms no more. There are no buds, no flowers. As if it's exhausted its empathy. Yet, from now on, a rose follows me. Fuchsia or red, one appears in the most unlikely of places, at the most unexpected of moments. And while there's no rose today, one white lotus blossoms forth on the far-corner pond. In his ever-kindly way, Ketut tells us it means "growth". Hindu tolerance and receptivity see beauty rising out of muddy waters. Me? I cannot imagine any growth. I feel like a stubbed-out cigarette, crushed underfoot. Extinguished.

I'm so wrung out that I feel like doing nothing at all, but there are still obligations to attend to before taking the plane tomorrow night for Brisbane. This wasn't how Albert and I had planned leaving Bali. We were meant to have left ten days ago, returning to a magic little international film festival we frequented for some years over a June long weekend in La Foa village, north of Noumea, before returning to our island home.

Instead, Jeremy and I now have two specific missions. One turns out to be fruitless, the second more successful.

We, all three, including Ketut guide, driver-cum-friend now riveted to us by force of circumstances, return to the Honorary German Consulate in Sanur once again, convoked to return with the official registry office paper. We are in possession of the official yellow page stamped, signed, legible in English, from the crematorium funeral director. We believe it's the paper they had summoned us to bring. Alas, the two girls in the office won't accept it. They tell us we have to go Gianyar or Denpasar to a real registry office. Time is ticking over. Bureaucracy looms ahead. Where exactly? Phone number? What to do? They hardly budge. Can find no phone number. They eventually write down two addresses. Ketut steps in. As he put it, his "eyes turned red". In the face of such confrontation, the Indonesian girl finally gives in, saying they could stamp Albert's passport – which we'd also come for!

With a resounding thud, she pounds the stamp *UNGULTIG* – (i.e. *NOT VALID*) - on the inside page. Then, with a snip of scissors like an executioner's axe, her young German colleague cuts off the bottom corner of the plastified, identity page. Albert's well-travelled passport, witness to our sojourns in Japan, South Korea, Macau, Vietnam, Istanbul, Jordan, St Petersburg, Europe, Australia and New Zealand, is assigned to an end.

We get out of that dismal, unwelcoming, dull brown office as fast as we can. Fifty metres further away, we sit on the sea wall. Breathe five minutes of sea air. Think of Albert floating in his other world, the ocean, the Bali Sea. A world that requires no papers. A world where creatures blend harmoniously.

In one last effort to regularise papers, we return, not to Ubud, but to Gianyar, to the district registry office that Ketut knows. This pleasant, Ubud district capital town is becoming distinctly familiar. The queue for advice is not long, although all three of us nearly collapse on the floor when the seat we take gives way beneath us, prompting us to laugh, as we manage quite often to do. The congenial girl at the counter gives us a paper in Bahasa to fill in and explains the documents required, as well as visits to three officials – the head of Ketut's village, the district and the province. There's no way we can do all that in 24 hours. We ditch the whole idea and head "home".

Back at the hotel, I have a swim and Jem enjoys a Bintang. He's poured a glass for me. Just rinsed and slightly refreshed, I sit down to join him, still in my bathers. For some reason I decide to open the iPad. Kind emails have been flowing in since I announced Albert's departure, and especially since my account of his ceremonial cremation. I scroll down and there's the dreaded heading "Ni P" once again! And in paler script as the introduction to the message, in the left-hand column, flash the words: "We're coming to the hotel". I read no further. My heart starts racing, again. The hospital clerk is coming to the hotel! "Let's get out of here Jem, and go and eat."

No sooner had I said that, than there she was, an apparition, advancing along the path towards our verandah. "Mrs. Hilary. I'm P." Of course I recognised her. She continued, "This is our marketing manager." Gone was her former aggressiveness. I quickly wrapped my pool towel around me – not the most elegant way to receive the hospital accountant who had been hounding me for payment after payment. The reason for the bombshell visit: two identical, shopping-style printed bags, filled with double issues of all the hospital papers and clearances in order that we may leave the country tomorrow. Wow. Some consideration at last. A sigh of disbelief. Thank you. Good-bye.

While our trip to Sanur was inconclusive this morning, we've set ourselves another task that seems equally a hurdle and we have no idea as to its outcome. We would like to find elegant, dignified containers for the small boxes of ashes, and then distribute them by post. There will be one to Albert's daughter in Switzerland, one to me on Isle of Pines to cover the eventuality of possibly having it confiscated, and the third one that I'll attempt to carry in my hand luggage -- passing out of customs in Indonesia, then in and out of customs in Australia, and eventually in through customs in New Caledonia. All the regulations are an unknown. We'll try. Jeremy offers to go shopping. He returns indeed with three attractive, patterned aluminium square boxes that he inveigled a shopkeeper to separate from clusters of boxes, a bit like

Russian dolls, one inside the other. We package them up, ready for a trip to the post office tomorrow.

This evening, we deliver Albert's suitcase to Ketut at home. He can use it as a tool box while building a studio to rent to visitors, on what was once a handkerchief-sized spot of grass. We've accepted his invitation to his compound's weekly *Kecak* dance presentation. A few rows of visitors, 40 or 50 people, have come to watch ritualised enactments of mythological love stories and a trance-like fire dance. Suddenly there's an eruption of more dancers than visitors, all male of varying ages, all bare breasted and often breast-bone thin, clad only in their temple, black and white knee-length sarongs and red waist sashes. They sit, cross-legged, in widening circles, their chants, claps and gracious movements mesmerising us. Several exquisitely-dressed women and a child flit in and out as spirit dancers, before the final coconut-husk horseman fire dance. An hour's exhilaration. In keeping with our finales, Jeremy's phone dies – he has no photos, just reconciliation for our own spirits.

Friday 7 July: Our last day. A day when everything goes right. There's even a rose. But not at all where one usually finds a rose. Our task today is to post the two little boxes. We find the Ubud post office, indicated by a tiny sign down a side road, and a shop next door where we imagine we'll find bags or boxes to mail. Not at all. It's simply a convenience store. We inquire at the post office counter and are guided through a room where three fellows are playing chess via the television, to a back, garage-like, storeroom. "He'll make the boxes for you." The box-maker is a professional! With a cutter, some cast-off cardboard and a roll of large, brown tape, he goes about making two tightly-sealed boxes with precision.

We return to the counter to fill out two simple forms. Contents? Ashes! Value? N.C.V. The girl understands perfectly. Price? Express will be around $40, normal around $15. We opt for the latter. There's no hurry. *Ouf*! As the French say. So smooth, so easy, no trouble. That's a weight off our shoulders.

It's now late morning. There are almost no tourists around. We stroll along the main street to the multi-boothed, multi-storied market, then make our way to Ubud's long-established, well-known Café Wayan – a delight anytime of day or evening. Little paths through luxuriant tropical plants lead to numerous, almost hidden, canopied wooden daises for two to six people. We sit, almost lie, on long cushions, have coffee and while away an hour or so, waiting out a heavy midday rainstorm.

Soothed, shaken, but more relaxed than any time in the past week. Continuing in that vein, we treat ourselves to a Balinese massage at Sang Spa, then sit at the hotel bar and let Jaya pamper us with a glass of wine and a proper meal before leaving with Ketut at 5 p.m. for the International Airport.

We return our key to the hotel reception. Many thanks dear Ubud Inn staff for your kindness, gentleness, empathy and sympathy. All, each one, has experienced life's difficulties. Nyoman lost his wife three years ago in a scooter accident. They wish us well, and repeat, taking my hands in theirs, "Be strong". Then joining their hands in front of them in prayer, bid us "Farewell".

Deliberately, we set off early with Ketut. Our plane is not till after 10 o'clock this evening. The trip usually takes an hour. This time it's almost 40 minutes before we even get out of the Ubud town centre. The traffic is blocked everywhere. Ketut, as he's able, ducks more traffic jams by driving through the silver-making town, Celuk, and wood-carving Mas, but from Sanur onwards, it seems that every vehicle in Bali is on the road. Finally we reach the airport. It's 7.30 p.m., dark and raining. We leave Ketut tearfully. We could have done nothing, and nothing so beautifully, carefully, without him. Part of Albert will stay with this wiry, sensitive Balinese and his family.

We wait till around 8 p.m. for our departure check-in area to flash up. D-16. Now begins the series of security checks. My heart is in suspension. What of the little box in my carry-on bag and of Albert's passport? With Ketut and Jeremy, we've already decided that I won't make any sign or mention of it. Here goes!

The first security check – all bags, iPad inside OK – clear. Next – ticket check-in. It's quiet around us. There are few people. Remarkable is one Argentinian couple with Calvin Klein suitcases piled high, and accompanied by their hotel bell-boy. We seem small and "lightish". We're approached by a security man. "Please open your suitcase." He tests each one with a sort of pistol, for explosives! Again OK. "Tickets please." Jeremy already has his seat. 26D. I ask to sit next to or near him. The girl says he doesn't have a seat. "Yes, I do – see my phone." Then comes: "And Mr. Thoma? He's travelling with you?" My jaw drops. Now what? I mumble, "No, he has died." She batters not an eyelid, continues calmly checking us in, giving us D and F, leaving E a space in-between. My bag holding all the hospital papers weighs 19.9 kilos. The clerk attaches a "HEAVY. BEND YOUR KNEES" label. Jeremy's is only 16.5 kilos – all fine.

But we're not done yet. There's another security check for hand luggage; out comes the iPad. All goes through, no stopping, no questioning. As I tidy my carry-on bag, I notice the screen-watching staff chatting, laughing amongst themselves. Three girls and a young man. One girl has a long-stemmed red rose that she's passing between them. It's wrapped the same way as ones sold in restaurants. Picking up on the relieved, lighter atmosphere, I ask if it's from a lover? They laugh. And spontaneously the girl closest to me gestures -- "Would you like it?" I couldn't believe it. "That's *very* special to me," I say, trying not to reveal my overwhelming emotion.

So I continue my way, carrying a red rose for Albert. Would it help me through the beckoning passport control? Would they see that Albert should be travelling with me? There's almost no queue. "One by one" reads the sign. I hand over my passport; rose in hand. The customs officer looks at it. He raises his eyebrows to check my resemblance, stamps it. Returns it. We're through! I still have the silver box, Albert's passport *and* a rose. No questions. The next step will be passing through Australian customs. Here, still in Indonesia, our good day Friday continues. We board the plane, exhausted, a little elated when we sit three in a row – Jeremy, the rose and me.

EIGHT

Swiss national colours

*Every life is an adventure navigating between
the unforeseen and the unexpected.*

François Cheng

To my unexpected relief, the small, square, silver box of ashes got the nod and a tolerant smile each time from customs and quarantine officers in and out of Australia, and then on into New Caledonia. Shortly after, the second box arrived intact, unquestioned, in my letter box.

Now, what to do with them? I unwrap them from the packaging and place them, as if on an altar, on the small, round, bronze table in my office lounge.

On returning home, I went almost immediately to discuss a memorial ceremony for Albert with the priest, Father G. On a separate occasion, I paid my respects to the High Chief, offering him a custom gift and explaining Albert's cremation. As a 47-year-long resident of the island, and being his senior by several years, the High Chief often referred to Albert as "*l'ancien*" (the elder). Island deaths and burials are highly ritualised in this traditional Melanesian-cum-Catholic society. Now confronted with an already-held cremation, the established ways have been thrown into disorder.

My thoughts were to hold a memorial day on 1 August (appropriately Swiss National Day), with a Mass, then a small ceremony at the cemetery on the hill above the church, followed by a lunch. (In past years, we had often shared a *raclette* with friends to celebrate the day when, back in 1291, three cantons united to form Switzerland.)

I suggested that there would be more meaning if those assisting would wear red or white or both. Father G took up the idea straight away. Instead of the usual purple vestments for mourning, he would opt not to wear red. "That's for martyrs," he quipped, but to wear white – an honour that Albert would appreciate. He would also mention my red and white wish in the church notices. Life and death on a Pacific island are not the same as in organised, sanitised, commercial towns and cities. "Farewelling" a member of the community is a hands-on, participative affair. Which means the family and clan not only digs the actual hole, usually for a locally-made coffin, but also chooses the actual burial site in the cemetery, often in family clusters. Father G suggested that Albert's remains be placed not too far from the entrance, somewhere near the final resting spot of the island's pioneering priests, who too, had spent several decades on the island. To this end, I was to climb up to the cemetery with two brothers who've been almost family to us for years, working not only in the diving business, but also in "cruise ship welcomes" for more than 30 years. So I made a rendezvous with Jean-Louis and Léon to do just that. But Jean-Louis was uncomfortable. He revealed to me that Albert had confided in him, saying when he died he wanted his ashes scattered at sea, returning to the silent world he so loved and that had brought him to, and kept him on Isle of Pines nearly five decades. It was a milieu that he had been introduced to through Jacques Cousteau's 1956 film, and for which he lived passionately, beginning in the Aeolian island, Lipari.

"Don't worry", I reassure Jean-Louis, "I have two boxes. We'll have another ceremony."

Jean-Louis arrived at the house early on the day of our arranged reconnoitre. "There's no need for you to go up to the cemetery", he told me. "Leon and I have been and chosen the spot for *Tchitchu* ('Jesus')", as most islanders always called Albert. How relieved I was. The chosen spot took on another dimension when he gave me more details. It was to be next to *Lélé* (Etienne), a person we'd appreciated from the days when he was our right-hand man, boat crew, entertainer, free-diver and genuine friend in the early days of the diving business in the early and mid-1970s. Incongruous it may seem, this bushy-bearded hunk had once pronounced to me, if anything happened to Albert, he'd take me for his wife! He left this world, still a young man, at the turn of the century. Now both gentle giants were to lie side by side. Close by, lay *Lélé*'s father, *Jean la Pipe* (John, the pipe-smoker). John was an affable man, a former merchant sailor on nickel trading boats, and who did indeed constantly smoke a pipe. Albert would be in familiar company.

I puzzled over how I was going to arrange to have a cross made. This was resolved by former diving partner and skilful woodworker, Tony, offering to make one out of a piece of *kohu*. Poignantly, this was not any old slab of the noble island wood, but one that had been recovered from our diving boat, *Toum-Toum,* that had sunk on one of the island's treacherous reefs back in 1985. This was the beloved, 50-year-old wooden cutter we'd all put so much into, physically, financially and in creating fond memories for divers. Had it come back to laud Albert? Had the circle come full circle? *Whatever*. It seems there's a reason for everything.

I wanted 1 August to be the least morbid possible. Albert was not a morbid or negative person. He loved life. He wouldn't approve of dirges or long, woeful eulogies. For several days I ruminate over what music would suit the mass ceremony. I listen to various requiems. They're all heavy, slow, sad. We're sad enough. I don't want music or hymns that add to the sadness. In the end, for the entrance, I choose Dvoràk's *New World Symphony No. 9*. Not traditionally sacred music, but not profane either. Eleven minutes of haunting, sometimes wistful, power and jubilation overcoming trepidation at moving to a new world; the way Czech Dvoràk did when he went to the U.S.A. in the 1890s, and the way Albert did when he moved from Switzerland to New Caledonia at the other end of the world, in 1970.

(Albert first set off by train for Moscow, in the days of the Iron Curtain and few travellers, before flying to Vladivostock, then to Yokohama by boat; plane to Sydney, Noumea and eventually Isle of Pines – all for less than the price of an air ticket in those days.)

Handel's *Alleluia*, sung with resonating richness by the island's church choir, would fittingly close the ceremony. I leave it to them to choose several hymns in-between.

They collaborate, with sensitivity, to the point of all wearing red shirts or red and white mission dresses for the occasion. Other mourners will also participate in the same way, creating a harmony and solidarity unusual, for western funerals at least, by not wearing black, and unusual here where multi colours reflect everyday Melanesian dress. Three close photographer friends will fly from Noumea to be by my side for the day. In front of our pew, a small, memorial table to the left of the altar will be draped in white. There, before the ceremony, I lay the square, silver box of ashes, awaiting the priest's blessing. Beside them I place Albert's trademark, white panama hat, a small sculpture of a diver made from nuts and bolts, and an industrial reel of white cotton, representing his past 30 years as a beach-wear designer and producer. Our garden provides me with one last stem of a tiny, red rose to carry.

Tuesday 1 August 2017. A gentle dawn. A few fluffy clouds in an otherwise pristine sky. An almost summer day in the height of our Southern Hemisphere, Tropic of Capricorn, cool season. Leidy, a long-time friend who's kindly come to stay with me for a few weeks, drives us to the village. I'm unused to being a passenger. Albert never had a licence. It all seems unreal.

After the mass, the solemnity continues. The cortege, lightened by not having to shoulder a heavy, cumbersome coffin, makes its way up the bamboo-lined hill behind the church to the cemetery. Father G, slightly older than Albert, cedes his place to acolyte, Théo, who's also Jean-Louis' and Léon's brother – it's all in the family. I close the ranks, having taken time to talk with various islanders on the church steps. By the time I arrive, Jean-Louis and Léon are lining the shallow hole (about half a metre deep), with lengths of colourful island material. Deacon, Théo, is beginning prayers. The setting, at the foot of a towering double-trunked, araucaria pine, is worth a painting.

In turns, the assembly pay their homage one by one, pausing to offer a prayer and a thought over the blessed little rattan box that was inside the silver box, many tossing in the bouquet they carry, before several men volunteer to spade in the surrounding earth, forming a slight mound on which they then place the *kohu* cross, engraved simply:

Albert Thoma 01.05.1934 – 30.06.2017

47 *ans à l'Ile des Pins*

"Je pense avec mes mains."

(47 years on Isle of Pines "I think with my hands.")

The closing line was Albert's catchword, a tribute ennobling manual skills. By inscribing that for posterity, I hope younger people who pass this way may be inspired to consider the importance of learning and using manual trades.

We've said our symbolic *au revoirs*. The day, late morning, is bright, still and warm. We make our way down from the top of the rise overlooking Vao village, catching glimpses here and there of the bays beyond St. Joseph Bay, and, straight ahead, to the renown atoll, Nokanhui, and further out into the ocean, the Pacific.

Lunch, so thoughtfully organised by lodging owners, Guillaume and Eulalie, and manager, Nicholas, and staff, reflects the Swiss colours. It turns out to be as if a garden party, in a wooded, grassy park usually reserved for campers. We raise our glasses, in courtesy and respect, to the absent, honoured guest, uppermost in our minds. For the cuisine, we've chosen a traditional *Bami,* denoting more than a century of Javanese migration to New Caledonia, a chicken, peanut-sauce *satay* popular in Bali, fruit platters, including tiny batons of fresh sugar-cane to chew on, followed by coffee and chocolate. The clan leaders under whose watch we come, present a small, custom ceremony, offering us yams and bolts of material, before closing the gathering by planting a *bugny* tree in Albert's memory. The *bugny* is a highly respected tree amongst Melanesians. Its fine-grained, dense wood, reputable for turning. The most well-known grove of *bugny* trees in the country grows in an arching avenue along Kanumera Bay, just two minutes from our home.

A pleasant idea was launched by Roger, a friend from when he and his ten siblings and parents (his father was an auxiliary *gendarme*) lived next door to us when we built our house. Should anyone wish to remember

Albert, it was suggested that they plant a tree of their choice in their own garden. Roger and his wife instigated the idea by planting a *pomme canaque* (a kanak apple tree) – a local, distant relation to an apple tree, in that the soft flesh fruit is pink on the outside and white inside. The couple was chuffed to hear Albert was indeed partial to apples, to the point where he grated one every morning to mix with his bowl of oats (*Uncle Toby's*), milk and a sprinkling of *Milo*. This he preceded by a large slice of ripe papaya, eaten contemplatively 'neath the banyan tree in our garden. Was that part of the secret of his long, solid life? The suggestion is not mine, but that of a friend who detects earth's positive and negative energies using a pendulum. At 12,500 Bovis Units, the ground beneath our banyan tree radiates good vibes verging on the sacred. Call it pseudo-science or authentic verification, we've always felt protected by the spreading aerial root system, as if we're enveloped in nature's arms or the embrace of a cathedral.

Our three photographer friends, who had come from Noumea for the day, ended it in the same commemorative way, planting a young, sprouting coconut in front of the red-door cinema Albert built in our garden 14 years earlier. The metal construction that he and Jean-Louis built in 12 days is a reminder to us of the force of nature. They finished it just one week before Cyclone Erica ripped into Isle of Pines, its 200 km per hour winds shearing away the roof of our kitchen and lounge, but leaving the new cinema intact.

NINE

Swirling waters of widowhood

When you are sorrowful, look again in you heart, and you will see that in truth you are weeping for that which has been your delight.

Kahlil Gibran

Life as a couple for 42 years was a tranquil river. The occasional ripple, one or two storms, but mostly gently flowing. Then – wham. Death snuffs out the other. You're all alone. You fall out of the river, over the edge, into the whirlpool of rapids way below. The spinning, the nothingness, the unknowingness begins. I write to a friend: "Nothing equips us Westerners to cope with the slam-bang brutality of losing one's partner of several decades". Nothingness swallows everything. There's no sense to anything anymore. No reason for being. I feel gouged out from mouth to stomach pit. It's a nauseous feeling that stays with me months on end. A weird feeling. One I've never experienced before. "It's called 'heartache' ", consoles an understanding friend.

New Zealand paediatrician, Diana Mason, spoke in the same vein when her playwright husband, Bruce Mason, slid from coma into death. She spoke of travelling aimlessly, of the "aching void that might have surprised even him, and that nothing – no music, no golf, no family, no friends – ever fills". The flamboyant, deliverer and carer of babies, concluded, however, that she would thank God, in whatever years left to her, for her "unquenchable belief in the power of the life force".

I too, feel that force, whatever it may be, that somehow propels me along, as if a magnet, from one day to the next, one day at a time. That force that acts as a buoy, when one would otherwise probably sink, go under, let the rapids wash one under.

When you are bereaved, at your most fragile, administrative papers pile up, bombard the remaining, living partner with callousness devoid of empathy. It all becomes an insurmountable wall that takes constant battering before making the slightest dent.

"Stories that end tidily and happily don't exist in real life. That's just fantasy." wrote John Hodgman in his foreword to the illustrated edition of George R.R. Martin's, *A Game of Thrones*.

It was for me, as the Queen so well expressed, in her annual 1992 speech to the nation, the year Charles and Diana separated, "... not a year on which I shall look back with undiluted pleasure ... it turned out to be an *annus horribilis*".

Throughout the horrible year, I've felt like a bird with a broken wing. Breathing, blinking, eating to survive, fluttering in the same spot. Nature might repair itself, but I've come to learn professional help also aids the healing. It would never have come of my own initiative. The idea would never have crossed my mind. I would never have dared entertain the idea. But a wise, gentle friend suggested just that – that I seek counsel outside my realm of usual acquaintance. Frankly, the world of psychotherapy was an unknown to me. I had a stereotyped impression that it was for the deranged. And anyway, what would I say?

Reluctantly, I accepted the advice. It turns out that the experience has been another learning curve for me. I have a new-found respect for the profession's practitioners. I'm in admiration of their capacity to be sounding-boards, to absorb others' woes and to help someone feeble come out the other side of the tunnel with a little more courage. My broken wing is mending. I'm nearing flying low, but I'm staying in the air.

And yes, there's a reason for everything. One year after my returning to Isle of Pines, almost to the day, I badly sprained my right knee, twisting it 90 degrees. Wow. The pain! I was incapacitated in terms of moving around. I learnt to use crutches, wearing a full-length leg brace, night and day for a couple of weeks, and finding myself suddenly beholden to the kindness of neighbours and friends, not only for meals, but even the ritual of taking a shower. The armour I had steeled myself within over the past year disappeared. The bravado I had presented to the outside world effaced. I was no longer independent, capable of getting along as well as possible.

The week before, I was on the ladder, pruning a handsome bougainvillea bush, and was just a couple of rungs from climbing on our roof. The next week, in one wrong step, an "unwatchful moment", I slipped on a stepping stone coming down off a ledge where I had reached to gather a green papaya. In two seconds, my independent, swim-every-day, do-everything-on-my-own person, was reduced to not moving, to accepting others' kind help and to re-thinking what is this fragile life.

Five weeks and ten professional massages later, I emerged, shedding the crutches, tottering as an infant must feel when it takes its first steps unaided. Several days after this five-week gap, I drove the car again, accompanied by a friend, just in case, and felt "liberated". I wanted to toot all the way along Kuto bay; I was independent again, whoopee! I was also a different person.

I'm now uncertain about the future. I'll stick to confronting each day as it comes - to seeing each day as a gift, each new person I meet as a gift, each person who is not new also, as a gift.

It is as if I have a delicate, new skin, the way a lobster sheds its shell and is pink and tender underneath. I realise that I'm vulnerable and need to protect myself. I need to go at my own pace. I need to learn how to be kind to myself, to practise "inner hospitality", the way Irish philosopher John O'Donohue suggests.

And it has been a lesson. Perhaps a lucky lesson. A lesson that I'm not 21 anymore. That I should probably keep my feet on the ground instead of blithely climbing the ladder, or mounting a high stool to put up the curtains. That I should learn to ask younger, more lithesome people for help. My "Patea Momma", my paternal grandmother, fell off a stool and broke her hip. Three months later she left this life and her dear husband. Three months later, he followed her. I tell myself I should now remember that and, reluctantly, be careful.

TEN

A designer life

I've lived a life that's full
I've travelled each and every highway but more, much more than this
I did it my way.
Paul Anka for Frank Sinatra

Resonating, clichéd words from the Crooner himself, but nonetheless fitting.

For all the condolence messages laden with sympathy and sorrow I receive, few take a lighter, more positive, dare I say, celebratory slant. Months later, that lighter spirit still gladdens my heart. Cousin John, a Kiwi, who's lived in Japan almost as long as I've lived on Isle of Pines, wrote on 19 July 2017:

> So Albert went out in style! I'm very glad to hear that and it sounds as though it was an ending with which he would have approved. Not everyone gets to have a Hindu funeral ceremony in Bali …
>
> Dealing with all this in a foreign land must have been really tough, but you did it. I'm very impressed. And having sibling support to count on must have helped a lot. I guess these are the times when our families, loosey-goosey though they may be these days, kick in and really mean something.
>
> Of course this is sad to hear, but Albert would have been, what, 82(?) by now, so I guess it was the fullness of time. He and you did get to have an amazing sojourn together – and on your own terms.

Almost a designer life, from my perspective.

Thank you for sharing the news, and do keep us informed of your next moves.

Take it easy, and think positive! All the best, John & Kumi.

Yes, Albert's was a designer sort of life, figuratively and literally. He did what he liked and liked what he did. Son of a gold-leaf painter, he inherited artistic genes from a father who courted his mother for two years before her family approved their marriage, posting her once a week a miniature, post-card painting declaring his unwavering love, and that, in the same pretty, lake-side town they both lived, Zug, Switzerland. Albert was manual rather than academic, although he spoke four languages with ease. He started work at 14 as an apprentice graphic and interior designer. The four-year apprenticeship in Lucerne equipped him with skills not only to design window displays, such as for the Omega watch company throughout Switzerland, but to build exhibition stands and pavilions to the point where he was able to build our own house including all carpentry and electricity. Such work also trained him to plan well in advance, often working six months ahead on presentations and displays.

He didn't wander aimlessly through life. Every day had a purpose. He was disciplined and creative. The centre exposed roof beams in our sleeping bungalow, for example, are two coconut tree trunks; the bookshelves in our lounge hang from the ceiling rather than sitting on the floor. Our windows are long rectangles, horizontal or vertical, not square boxes. His was a designer's eye.

He bore out the observation by Canadian retirement expert and author, Barry LaValley, *The longer you work at something you like, the longer you live.*

Albert loved to work. It wasn't a chore. Even until the day we went on our last holiday to Bali, at 83 years of age, Albert still worked six days a week, designing, sewing and painting. His day was rhythmed by fairly set hours morning and afternoon, broken by our ritual stop around midday. A time to take a daily dip in the aqua waters of one of the two bays bordering the peninsula where we live, two of the most beautiful beaches in the South Pacific. Back in the days when he ran the diving business, tourism dictated that the week ran seven days. In his thirties in Switzerland he would often work at night, apart from his daytime graphic designer's job, so as to make extra money for diving holidays.

Lebanese writer, Kahlil Gibran, has some beautiful reflections on work: "Work", declares Gibran, "is love made visible. When you work you are a flute through whose heart the whispering of the hours turns to music....when you work you fulfil a part of earth's farthest dream, assigned to you when that dream was born,

And in keeping yourself with labour, you are in truth loving life,

And to love life through labour is to be intimate with life's inmost secret."

Albert was not negative, but there was one thing in New Caledonia he could not abide: the way the radio stations, presenters of all ilks, news as well as other programmes, make an idol of the weekend, denigrating and bemoaning the working week, restricting it Monday to Friday; along the lines, on a Monday morning: "Oh Monday, you had a good weekend?"; come Wednesday, "only two more days till the weekend", then come Friday, the elation at bordering on the weekend: "*Youpi* – Yippee! Friday!"

Albert found it disappointing that a little country possibly verging on independence should be indoctrinated with a distaste-for-work attitude. To him, it took away the pride and value of work by cultivating an anti-work ethic. For him, it was always not only the personal satisfaction of working and creating, but also the inner satisfaction of pleasing customers, whether they be divers, or visitors interested in a hand-painted beachwear item. Of course he worked for financial reward too, indeed that was why he gave away the diving, because a big, old wooden boat, underwater equipment and maintenance proved to be a guzzling hole for revenue.

In more recent years, each *paréo*/sarong or t-shirt was a kilometre or two further for our next voyage. Yet, recognising making money is a necessity to live and travel, it was nevertheless not a subject to be dwelled on, nor an end in itself.

An old Irish blessing reads:

May your work never weary you.

May it release within you wellsprings of refreshment, inspiration and excitement. May the day never burden.

May dawn find you awake and alert, approaching your new day with dreams, possibilities and promises.

May evening find you gracious and fulfilled.

May you go into the night blessed, sheltered and protected.

May your soul calm, console and renew you.

Yes, a certain spirituality guided Albert's work. Certainly he always had vision. Some of his innovations were not realised, although he had drawn up plans for them:

A museum, living and working, of the convict history here on Isle of Pines. The island hosted some 3000 political convicts from France in the 1870s, then other common law prisoners until 1912. There are still some abandoned stone buildings from that time that could have been saved more easily 40 years ago, than now, especially if each visitor to the island since had contributed just 100 francs (a little over a dollar). But there was no political will to back the project, from New Caledonia through to France.

A floating hotel, resembling a low, v-shaped catamaran, for divers in the sheltered waters at the north-west of the island; completely ecological, with recycled water, and cooperation from the tribe close by to provide fresh produce. But it ran into opposition from a couple of island elders and the idea was abandoned.

A golf course and small hotel converting an abandoned two-storey, 40-room building into a 20-studio boutique hotel. The *Relais de Kanuméra* hotel, straddling Kuto and Kanumera Bays, Isle of Pines, shut down in 1979 because of an outside financial dispute.

These projects of Albert, dreams turned disappointments, fell on unattuned ears; projects too modern for their time.

Some people dream. Some people talk, but not so many translate their dreams into reality. A *cinéphile*, movie-lover, from way back, Albert dreamed of watching movies in our garden on a big screen. We'd never had television in the house. So one day he did build a cinema in the garden. In twelve days he and Jean-Louis had fun soldering steel to erect a building to house the ceiling projector he'd saved for years to buy and thereby project DVDs onto a flat iron, white wall giving us a fabulous 3 x 4 metre picture in all simplicity. Five director's chairs, two bean bags and cushions – that's our cinema and now our connection to the outside world, as later, a small satellite dish enabled us to capture basic television channels from Noumea and thus, France.

Jazz was another of Albert's passions. It was a deep passion initiated by his listening to shortwave *Voice of America* and *BBC Radio* broadcasts during the second World War. He kept a program from his first jazz concert in Lucerne in 1952. The line-up of stars, jamming together that same night, was enough to form a convert for life and would make any jazz devotee of any generation drool: young Ella Fitzgerald, Ray Brown, Hank Jones, Oscar Peterson, Gene Krupa … names that became classics of jazz for all time, under the patronage of impresario Norman Granz, who presented them together that same year at Carnegie Hall. By good fortune, 51 years later, we stumbled upon Hank Jones playing at the famous, intimate jazz club, Birdland, in New York. Cake and candles marked his 90th birthday. Music in general accompanied Albert every day in the workshop. The radio or CDs beating out good rhythm and melody. French singer Patricia Kass was a particular favourite. He had most of her releases and almost wore down the CDs, if that be possible.

Jacques Cousteau, co-inventor of the underwater breathing apparatus or regulator, visited Isle of Pines around 1990, with a mutual diving friend and great story-teller, Riquet. At the time Cousteau would have been 80. I remember Riquet telling me Cousteau nurtured projects as if he was going to live another 20 years. Albert was the same. He always had projects. Work projects: he'd designed a new line of beach-wear, had worked on it for two years, had already made sample pieces (tried them on me and asked my opinion) and had planned on producing the range through the second half of 2017. Travel projects: he dreamed about crossing the Grand Canyon in a helicopter or hot-air balloon and had checked out corresponding hotels. Another travel date he'd ringed was the *Fête des*

Vignerons, a once in every 22 to 25 years pageant held in Vevey, Switzerland, where Béa, his daughter, lives, scheduled for the summer of 2019.

However, as a long-time friend and former ABC Radio colleague reminded me poignantly: "Man proposes, but God disposes"! That, she wrote, "was the salutary life lesson" emanating from "the momentous upheaval of events" that disrupted my life last June/July. Now, she continued, it's for me to gradually and carefully put the shattered pieces back together. A true and observant friend, her letter continued:

"I was reminded of the last two times we met up with you and Albert, one in London and the last in northern New South Wales, when you presented an ethereal presence of spring white garb – the pair of you seemed to float into our encounters, wraiths of filmy light. Perhaps some day, you'll consider organising a *Diner en Blanc,* where the guests wear only white and the men often sport panamas, such as Albert used to do with flair."

While I might not run to organising *Un Diner en Blanc,* given her encouragement and my starting to find my feet again, I might consider organising in December, a *Brunch en Blanc,* the way we traditionally did, year after year, approaching Christmas. More English than French, brunch 'neath our banyan tree, starting at 9, with champagne and orange juice, often intrigued and ultimately pleased our mostly French guests. December 2017 I could not entertain the idea at all. I had no heart nor enthusiasm to take Albert's place. This year, I'll see.

My confidant, friend and lover, he was not a saint. None of us are. He was a Taurus, with a bit of the devil thrown in. Nonetheless, I keep him on a pedestal. Tall, straight, blue-eyed. I keep his photo 'neath a rose in a single stem vase, light a candle or two every evening and raise my glass to thank him for our decades together.

As English actress, Joyce Grenfell wrote:
Parting is hell, But life goes on, So sing as well.

Our rose.

Jeremy and Albert.

Kou-Bugny Hotel, Kuto, January 2017 (photo courtesy E. Dell'Erba).

Ubud Inn, Bali, Albert's photo 20 June 2017.

Morning Offerings.

Albert's last photo of me, 19 June 2017.

In the same spot, 5 July 2017.

The Hindu-Balinese calendar that decided the cremation date.

Left to right: Ketut's parents-in-law, the author, Jeremy, Ketut's wife, Wayan, Ketut - before the cremation ceremony.

What can I say?

Brush Island, 2 January 2018.

Blue skies and the sea for company, for memories, Brush Island, 2 January 2018.

ELEVEN

Officialdom : Beware, be wary

*Never take **No** for an answer.*
The Small Miracle, Paul Gallico

An English friend who's lived both in New Caledonia and France swears she would never live in a French country again. For one reason: because it drowns its people, saps their morale, energy and initiative beneath an avalanche of paperwork. The smallest application, as mundane as a travel fidelity card, requires numerous proofs of identity: passport or identity card, an electricity bill, an attestation of residence. Questions or proof are understandable in a city of thousands or millions, but when one lives on an island of 2000 people, where everyone knows everyone, it really pushes limits, apart from patience.

And now **a warning**! Die close to home, somewhere where those left behind speak the language, can navigate papers and administration. If you have any choice, try not to die as a foreigner in a foreign land. And **beware**! Be wary! If you blithely, in all good faith, buy travel insurance and sail off/fly off nonchalantly to a foreign destination, check the finest small print before thinking for one second that you have wrapped yourself in comfortable protection, that some company will come to your aid when you desperately need their advice and real help.

In our case it was total rebuff. That was my experience from the first day Albert was hospitalised. The worldwide company from which we had bought travel insurance for years, dropped us like a hot cake from Day One. The Paris bureau, nominated as the contact in the standard brochure issued with the insurance receipt, referred our case to the Noumean office where we had paid the insurance. That office glibly replied that, initially, we would have to pay. Settlement would first need to be made through our local health cover. Then, the insurance would pay the complement. And, in the meantime? Faced with the horror of the unknown, the looming hospital bills and more of the unknown, we, as naïve clients, could look after ourselves. And that's what happened. No heart. No empathy. No explanation or excuse from the travel insurance office as to why they would not take the financial responsibility straight away. I did not understand then, and I still do not understand on what pretext the insurance company refused to take responsibility for our bills immediately, when it stipulates in the policy: *"Hospitalisation. An unforeseen stay of more than 48 hours, in a public or private care establishment, for medical or surgical treatment following a grave bodily attack whose occurrence was not known to the beneficiary in the five days prior to its apparition."* The hospital too, as standard practice, advised and requested financial intervention from the insurance company. To no avail.

We never imagined for one second, when buying the insurance, that the company would take stalling measures invoking social security payments first, and their paying "the complement" second. From Day One I realised that people in offices, responsible for paying out money that is not their own, are devoid of compassion. Possibly I'm not cynical enough to think that stalling measures mean a company continues to collect interest on money for more than a year, that they might otherwise have paid out earlier. Fifteen months later, the battle continues. "They, the health cover, will settle, then we'll pay the complement", reiterates the travel insurance spokeswoman.

I ask myself: What if we didn't have savings and family to pay the bills? Bills that stood no delays. Bills that had to be paid on the spot. What would have happened to us? Would Albert have had to suffer the indignity of sitting on a bench, in the tropical heat, in his agony, awaiting treatment from the "poor people's hospital". And then? Would we have had to offer him a pauper's funeral for want of ready funds?

It took me three months to find out that the place I'd seemingly lodged the papers for Albert's official death certificate was not correct. In fact, the girl in the local council office hadn't even sent them away to what she thought was the right court office until a week before, when a kind friend started asking hard questions. She'd been sitting on the papers, almost literally, and to my infrequent inquiries kept replying "Oh, it'll take a loooonnng time." That way it could have taken forever.

As it was, it took a year! Noumean authorities, I found out eventually, were not involved. It turned out the Indonesian Consulate in Noumea however was kind and helpful. I had to obtain copies of passports from two witnesses who were with us in Bali, had to fill out question upon question, including Albert's birth certificate and the names of his parents, and send all documents to the registry office of the Ubud district capital, Gianyar. That I did and sent off with a sigh, on December 31 2017. Goodbye 2017.

Over the next few months I inquire, I inquire. I wait and I wait. Finally, on 4 July 2018 (Independence day! American), I receive an email from the kind Indonesian consulate assistant in Noumea. I had been told that the official death certificate could not be posted but would need to be collected in person! There was no way I could face returning to Bali on such a mission. It was to my relief then that I scrolled down the consulate assistant's lines; she had had a friend go to the Gianyar office and had brought it back to Noumea. The story was that the document was completed "a while ago" – I see it was dated: *The Twenty-ninth of January two thousand and eighteen*. It was now over five months later. The Gianyar office's explanation was that they didn't know where to send it by postal mail and didn't have a working scanner to send it by email. The kind apology read: "I am so sorry for the traditional obstacle, here in the digital era".

Until that July day, I'd started convincing myself that Albert hadn't (officially) really died, as I had no official confirmation, and probably never would have. Now having received the document, or at least its copy via email, I have to accept the cold fact, as it's written in black on a pale green background, the document decorated with beautiful Indonesian scroll work in red and green.

The official death certificate was one of the papers I'd been asked for by the health insurance. The enormity of French administrative paperwork (after all New Caledonia is still French at the time of writing, and its institutions modelled on French ones), raises one's hackles, chokes even. *Rest in Peace* is not a byword for French administration. One comes to the feeling that it's easier to be alive than dead for the deceased person. And that there's no rest for the already suffering persons left behind. Often one has the feeling there's little communication between the director of this, and the-officer-in-charge of that. A lexicon of unkind adjectives swells up in the face of such intimidation – nasty, for example, vicious, pernicious ….!

Apart from being unaided by our travel insurance company when I needed them most, the next officialdom kick in the teeth I received, once home, was startling and unexpected. Furthermore it was not officially legal, but operates widely, indeed is standard practice in France, although I was unaware of such action.

To explain: Albert and I each had, over several recent years, set aside francs in separate savings accounts to cover funeral expenses! We believed we were being responsible and forward-thinking, lightening the onus on whichever one it might fall.

Given that everything happened so quickly in Bali, when I returned home I decided to withdraw the sum in Albert's special account – I had official power of attorney. Imagine my surprise when the girl behind the counter, whom I know well, came with a set, snappy reply, "No, you can't withdraw anything. The account is blocked." Did I hear correctly? Who blocked it? I spurt out. Her reply was non-committal. So I asked to speak to her boss further up the line in Noumea. There was no getting past the telephone receptionist, who, when I pressed her as to who had blocked the account, she let out: "The Morgue! We can arrange payment with the morgue." Again, did I hear correctly? And how did the morgue know? Out she blurted the reply: *Les Nouvelles* – the News! It appears the morgue keeps an eye on all death notices. After all, morgue business is lucrative business and being ensured they're paid is apparently part of that business. Had I suspected such machination, I would never have asked a friend to place the death notice in the newspaper, *Les Nouvelles*. Now, every time

I read a death notice in the newspaper or hear a radio announcement, a daily practice here, I shudder. I shudder for the families involved and all the extra pain and sheer battles they will face. I informed the telephonist with whom I spoke that the morgue in Noumea had nothing to do with our situation. That it was dismally too late for any intervention on its behalf. That there was no need at all for any payment to be made there.

Well that stirred a hornet's nest. There was no way of unblocking the account. I even went as far as having a friend well-placed in the *Cour des Comptes* in France, a sort of National Audit Office, investigate the validity of such action. *His reply*: It was not legal until a death certificate was issued – which, as I've explained, came only one year later. However, as a rider, he added: Banks are not philanthropists. And sure enough, he was right. Refusal to unblock the sum, which would have just covered the steep funeral expenses, meant the obligation to seek a *notaire*, a notary public, a lawyer specialising in authenticating documents, who goes by the title of *Maître*, Master, if you please. All of which costs the client, the man in the street, the victim, dare I say. Banks, notaries, the morgue, would seem to go hand-in-hand.

One day, considerably later, during a lull at the agency where the account in question is, the clerk offered advice in hindsight: "You know what you should have done, was withdraw the funds immediately on Albert's death. Then, she added, there would have been no problem". Not only did I gasp at her disarming frankness, but I reiterated, firstly, I was thousands of kilometres away in Bali and, secondly, such a cold, calculating idea would never have crossed my mind. How perverse. How baseless and devoid of humanity a system that pushes its clients to act that way, in the most fragile moments of one's existence. Apparently, so goes the official rap, the action is to stop unlawful family members accessing a dead person's account.

Now I begin to talk around, broach the subject with other people. I find I'm not alone. The astute father of a family I know here on the island, sensing his own imminent passing-away, withdrew every franc from his account, that way kindly avoiding all discomfort and legal proceedings for his wife and children. One friend, close to my age, whom I hadn't seen for a several years, confirms the practice. She tells me she's instructed her son, to whom she has already given power of attorney to her bank account, that immediately on the death of herself or of her husband, despite his disarray and grief, he's to withdraw every franc from the account or accounts concerned. A vicious system summons up vicious responses. One would think official, written power of attorney would whittle down chances of abuse, but apparently French banks do not trust their written records. Or perhaps it's just another insidious way of putting more money in their coffers? In our case I have no idea whatever happened to the sum Albert diligently worked for and put away, thinking he was being responsible for his own funeral costs. In the least harmful situation, the sum will go to his daughter, minus the charges made by the notary; in the more disagreeable situation, the state will swallow the sum. As of fifteen months later, no person, no organisation, has ever replied to my questions or informed me of any outcome. Who pocketed the money Albert worked for?

Another brick wall. Another Beware, Be Wary warning the blocked account gave rise to, incorporates the question: when is a Will, not a Will? If you make a will, guided and signed by a lawyer, in one country, do not imagine that it will necessarily be accepted in another. That too has been my experience – the notary insisting that it does not comply with French inheritance rules. His also insisting on keeping the original for the archives. Bang. Slam. What's written is not what is to be understood or acted upon, even after having followed instructions to pay to have it officially translated. No. It's not valid. So what is a Will, if it is not a Will to be respected and in my humble opinion, out of respect for the deceased person concerned? This obstinacy, this no-leniency, causes more anguish, more incomprehension, more not-knowing-where-to-turn.

Banking world officialdom may be difficult to navigate, but European/French officialdom is often unfathomable. There's a word in French, *borné* (close-minded – stuck on one theme) and another, *têtu* (stubborn); put them both together in the confines of some public servants, unaccustomed to using initiative and the system impels you against a brick wall. It's interesting that the *En Marche* government in

France recognises its economy could be improved by paring down its civil service. That could be equally, if not more valid in New Caledonia, where one third of the workforce is in the employ of the state. Certainly, there are some wonderful state employees, medical and educational staff for example, but in many cases, being a public servant in any country translates in practical terms to creating and producing nothing. More often than not, their existence seems to dog the ones who really do work in a productive manner, keeping the wheels of industry turning.

Because I was refused immediate financial help from our travel insurance, their office was my first stop of call on returning to Noumea. I handed them the carry-all full of papers from the hospital. We'll handle everything, don't you worry, the girl assigned the dossier assured me. We'll deliver the papers to the health fund and will follow through. You will be paid. She didn't specify when. That "when" still hovers in oblivion 15 months later. I handed over all the papers for hospital, cremation and extended hotel stay to the insurance in good faith and now, what seems to me, total naivety.

I imagined the hospital papers were to concern reimbursement according to the full health cover Albert had. Later I requested that payment also cover the additional six months member charges they continued to deduct following Albert's death.

But I imagined wrongly. I was regularly hounded to prove that I was Albert's *héritière,* legatee, heiress. I didn't seek anything except that the six extra months charges be reimbursed to me. Instead, I receive an unsolicited form concerning reimbursement of payments made over decades. The unsolicited form indicates that a "conjoint" has rights to this. So too does the internet link they refer to, given there are no dependent children. But to prove that one is a conjoint, it is not sufficient for the department to look at their records and see that our payments were made jointly. No, the arrogance goes further. Given that we were not married (and Albert had his reasons, having been "once bitten, twice shy"), I had to prove in black and white, with an *Attestation of Concubinage* delivered by the island town council office. Demeaning, in my opinion. After numerous to-ing and fro-ing, having proved on paper that I indeed have the right to be Albert's successor to live and occupy our parcel of tribal land, the reply comes on 20 July 2018: "This is not sufficient. We now require proof stipulating you are veritably Monsieur's heiress". One would think the funds are their own.

And all the while, as long as this organisation blocks its payment, which I originally believed to concern the hospital charges, our travel insurance, hand-in-hand with "the system", refuses to budge and to pay. It's drip-by-drip wearing down, sapping one's morale and the will to fight for one's rights and dues. I almost replied immediately to the refusal I received this morning from Madame E., "I believe you are splitting hairs. Forget the whole dossier. Toss it in the bin. Just liberate me so I can once more approach the recalcitrant travel insurance".

Delaying tactics, I'd call them.

And then I go back to the beginning of this chapter. I remind myself of Paul Gallico's advice. And I say to myself: dig in your heels; try once again. So I question the health insurance: Please tell me on what grounds you are blocking the travel insurance payout? Lo and behold, in black and white, comes their reply: "We are not blocking the travel insurance reimbursement."

So who is kidding who? Who is stalling? Who is using my rightful money and earning interest on it? Who is wearing me down and hoping I'll just go away? Odd that this particular worldwide insurance company is one of the most profitable companies in France. Odd that insurance companies are often the owners of banks. And how do they make their money? By capitalising on unsuspecting little customers like us, who pay, who pay, time after time, out of a sense of responsibility for one's own wellbeing, only, in the last resort, to find it's an uphill battle, that none of these companies, be they private or public, like paying out. Yet they never complain when the client pays, and on a regular basis what's more.

And so, on 17 August 2018, I receive an email from another woman in the health cover department saying she's just been going through Albert's Bali hospital dossier. She dares ask: "Did you really pay? We need proof of your payment."

I beg your pardon! I cannot believe my eyes. I hold a conversation in my head: It is now more than a year later and you ask if I really paid. You obviously have no idea of the Indonesian system. How do you imagine I ever left the country if I hadn't paid the millions of rupiahs? What have you been doing with that dossier for over a year? In what corner has it languished gathering dust, your hoping I'd give up the fight? The dossier has all the bills. Instead of replying immediately, I decide to go calmly, to ask infamous Ni P at Kasih Ibu Hospital, if she remembers me, if she can provide a receipt for our long-ago payment.

But even that is not easy. Her reply comes, "Yes of course we remember you. But our accounts section is closed today. August 17th is our Independence Day. I will try to obtain this for you on Monday." True, 17 August 2018 marks the 73rd anniversary of Indonesian independence from 350 years of Dutch colonial rule. Given that Indonesians, and Balinese in particular, love feast days of all sorts, I can imagine the elaborate ceremonies throughout the country today. Of course I'll wait. It's becoming a habit. Monday comes. Bali is three hours behind New Caledonia. I wait. Tuesday comes. I wait. Wednesday, I send an enquiry to Ni P once again. "Oh sorry, comes her reply, we have a public holiday and your dossier needs to be retrieved from 'the warehouse', (I presume she means their archives), we'll try tomorrow."

Finally, on 23 August, I receive the clear receipt for the charge of rupiahs in their hundreds of millions. Zeros are not just the preserve of Venezuela, Indonesia too makes monetary conversion complicated with its string of zeros.

I sigh and forward the requested receipt to Madame U. What do I receive? An automated reply stating: "I will be absent from 23 August (that's today, I gasp), back on 10 September." Wham. The door is shut in my face. There's no polite thought for the customer. No alternative, as is the custom in Australia and New Zealand, to round out the automated reply by adding thoughtfully, "Please contact so-and-so in my absence". Once more I take this as arrogance, lack of service to the public and care for the well-being of customers. It presents no glimmer of humanity or empathy toward the member who pays his dues (usually deducted automatically two weeks before they are actually due). At least Madame U is absent for only two and a half weeks. Unlike her colleague, the one who informed me that they do not block the travel insurance payout. That particular person subsequently sent an automated reply, in early August 2018, saying "I'm out of the office until March 2019"! And while there was no mention of any specific person to contact in her absence, there was a general address in case of a complaint. Not exactly polite in my book. Just simply, I'm out of here, you, the customer can dither in limbo. Such rudeness, in my view, is enough to raise the hackles of the most patient of ordinary folk.

I have a suggestion. All office employees who deal with the public in delicate situations should be given training in psychology and sociology. They should be made to realise that every time they say "No Madam", "Come back again Madam", "You need another document to justify your request", they are digging the knife deeper into an already bare and unhealed wound. That they are only prolonging the healing and deepening the excruciating, bloodless pain. Could there not be public debate about service to the public in the "public service"?

Israeli medieval history professor, Yuval Noah Harari, turned philosopher/thinker and bestseller writer to the point he's now hailed as the thinker of the moment, suggests the world needs more debate and to open debate, he declares, we need to ask questions. In my opinion, it would be healthy if we could ask more questions. But many officers, do not like the public asking questions. Ever so often, their reply comes back, "That's how it is" and no questioning is tolerated. Could it be that schools no longer educate students to learn how to debate, literally. I was fortunate growing up in the Wairarapa Valley in New Zealand. A group of high schools ran debating clubs and competitions between each other. These mental sports encounters were not only good training for mental discipline and gymnastics, but also fun when your brain was challenged to defend a side you didn't personally go along with.

Needless to say, I have little respect for either organisation that I have battered against for more than a year. It would be helpful if they would take a leaf out the Australian experience following floods in Brisbane in

2013, when the Prime Minister, Julia Gillard, insisted insurance claims have a four-month limit placed on their being executed. Need I underline that I'll never take out travel insurance, or any other cover again, with the particular world-wide insurance company I've dealt with. Furthermore, I'll advise as many others as possible, to do likewise. In order to avoid a libel case, I've deliberately not named the company and have changed the initials of the employees referred to in this chapter.

TWELVE

Unexpected kindnesses

It has long been an axiom of mine,
that the little things are infinitely the most important.
A Case of Identity, Arthur Conan Doyle

Unexpected kindnesses from unexpected quarters.

I attribute my survival over the months, now just over a year, to surprises, spontaneous gestures that warm my heart and make me believe I should keep on going. They counter the cold, officious, mean-minded quagmire of officialdom.

They began with Ketut and Jeremy. They spring forth, or pop out quirkily, when least expected, sometimes from people I hardly know. They can be an islander who takes my shoulder and rubs my heart, whispering *Courage*, take heart, be brave. They can be the kind neighbour who offers to climb the hill to the cemetery in the village with me, early morning, to discreetly pay a visit to Albert's memorial, just the birds and whispering pines for company. They can be my MnM friends (their first names begin with M), both mothers of four little ones each, who find the time to bring dainty cakes and visit me to chat once a week in the beginning, just to ease the pain. They can be friends who offer me a hot bath, with flowers and candles, or a hot spa by the light of early evening, the pine trees silhouetted against a darkening sky. Such kindnesses soften the pain.

When I returned from Bali, my hairdresser in Noumea gifted me her much-appreciated service when I came to pay. How kind. How touching. We have no hairdresser on Isle of Pines, so her kindness was even more meaningful.

A friend of more than 20 years, who lives in Noumea, gave me three weeks of her time when I returned home, accompanying me to what I feared would be a resounding, empty house, but which took on some warmth with shared meals and tears.

A young barman, in-between jobs on the island, stopped by my house one day shortly after I arrived home. Did I have any odd jobs he could help me with? How extraordinary. How appreciated. He repaired a floor tile in the bathroom, cleaned my car, pruned some branches, and in exchange, appreciated the *papaya gratin* lunch he stayed to share.

It's intriguing how something sweet is soothing. In Bali I drank sweet ginger tea or hot chocolate.

Both were comforting, despite the heat. Back home I've had kind condolences in the form of honey from a local beekeeper, and delicious home-made, creamy, salted caramel spread from someone I hardly knew, but have come to know more since. A former cruise-ship company colleague stops by; her toddler hands me a blue-ribbon-tied little box of exquisite chocolates hand-fashioned in Noumea and enthusiastically helps untie the wrapping.

Christmas 2017 with my sister and brother and families in Australia underlined the unspoken, spider-web strength of family ties. They've been guardian angels. So too, have many other friends from near and afar. Old friends mean deep understanding and different conversations. Even the neighbours' dogs are understanding. Do they know, according to Chinese astrology, I'm a dog too? When I do my yoga in the garden early morning, they'll quite often steal up behind to lick my ear. When one day in the early days, I burst into full lament, they were on my doorstep, wondering what was going on, eyeing me quizzically as if in sympathy. Passing kindnesses, when the occasional visitor extracts my story within five minutes of our meeting, then leaves, giving me a hug. When one is fragile and alone, a hug from a stranger is a heart-warming, unexpected small kindness.

Then there's the kind independent nurse who calls spontaneously at 11 a.m., on her Sunday day-off, inviting me to lunch, when I'd had a particularly sad morning and couldn't even swallow my breakfast.

In the first few months when it was hard for me to stay at the dining table and even in the house, my steps would take me aimlessly outside, down the road, through the stone wall and along the water's edge in Kuto, near the little wharf. One morning, overwhelmed with feeling sorry for myself, I sat on the steps leading down to the water. My head cupped in my hands, a feeling of nothingness and worthlessness. What appeared in front of me? A turtle raised its head out of the water close by, as if to say you're not alone. Then a lady who owns a taxi drove by and sang out *Bon dimanche Cléo*. (Have a pleasant Sunday Cleo.) Tiny gestures, but enough to shake me, lift my spirits. And then, that same time, in the next five minutes an acquaintance, who lives on a yacht in the bay, rode up in his dinghy, inviting me to his daughter's forthcoming communion and family dinner gathering. So, I shake myself, pick myself up and wander home with a lighter step. I'm not alone after all.

One evening, sitting forlorn on the same water's edge steps, I watched a fishing boat gently nudge into the wharf and disembark its iceboxes and gear. A vehicle and several people from the nearby hotel came to assist. I vaguely watched. Then I see one of the staff walking along the wharf swinging a good-sized, some 50-60 cm, fish by the tail. He comes on to land, then approaches me, holding out the fish, "This is for your dinner, it's from the boss"! I could not believe it. There I was, miserable, sad, alone. And I walk home carrying, in outstretched arms, the weighty, shimmering, elegant *saumon-des-dieux*. Half for the neighbours, in return for their filleting the rare, deep-sea treat, half for me for several meals.

A friend returns from holidays, finds me not at home, leaves a note written on a tissue tucked in the door, and a small, painted tin of buttery biscuits from her homeland in Brittany. At the village market, a lady selling fruit and vegetables slides me a ripe papaya; a girl who was one of my students, offers me an outsize, emerald bunch of parsley; another day, a lady I dealt with for cruise ship arrivals, grabs my arm, bends down into her basket, pulls out a ripe hand of sought-after bananas. Small, heart-warming gestures.

When I sprained my knee, the doctor on duty, handing me crutches, inquired how was I going to manage on my own. "I don't know," I sputtered out, not having given any thought to the consequences of my accident. Yet, out of the blue, unexpected kindnesses multiplied. Our closest neighbour, who's not a spring chicken, took it upon himself to bring me breakfast for the first ten days. And not just any breakfast, but caringly-prepared fresh orange or mandarin juice, followed by my ritual muesli, yoghurt and tea. His wife brought me beautifully presented meals most evenings, in the beginning. Friends and other neighbours rallied around, and I even managed to run the boutique ensconced on the divan, excusing myself to visitors and asking them to rustle in a box here or there for a t-shirt or a *paréo*.

The yachting friend who stopped by when I was still on crutches and caught me muttering out loud that I felt I needed a "square meal", a steak would do! It was after six, dark, windy. With no hesitation, he offered, "I'll take you to eat, this evening. Let's call the hotel." Call, we did. Cajoled a bit for a booking. He then picked me up crutches and all, drove my car along the bay and lo and behold, we had an excellent, spontaneous meal.

My sprained knee incident and subsequent learning aligns with Japanese writer, Haruki Murakami's experience when he had an accident on his bike because he failed to look where he was going. In his delightful essay, *What I talk about when I talk about running,* he warns philosophically, "Once you've had a scary incident like that, you really take it to heart. In most cases, learning something essential in life requires physical pain."

That's how my time since Albert's departure has been, exacerbated by my two seconds of inattention. Pain. Physical pain. July 7 2018, I jotted in my notebook:

A year ago today, Jeremy and I left Bali with a rose for Albert. Today, I swim under a pale blue, midday sky in waters typical of this cool time of the year. Sometimes at the beach, I used to say to myself, one day I'll be on my own, but I never imagined the pain.

Living on an island is a bit like living on a sailing yacht. One has to do everything oneself. That applies particularly to repairs and maintenance. Albert was an expert at keeping all in order. Now it's up to me. But while I can wield a hammer and a paint-brush, I'm not a fix-it-person. One day recently, I cautioned a couple wandering in to the boutique, not to touch the sliding door. I was worried about its sticking more and more, and couldn't fathom out the reason. "Let me take a look," said the tall Kiwi yachtie. "That needs re-hanging. The steel bar atop is not holding." Within a flash, he set off to his boat and returned, not only with his own tool kit, including electric drill, but with a mate. The two of them put their heads together, analysed the problem, worked on it and, half-an-hour later, *ouf*, the heavy door wobbled no more. The next day, to my dismay, I had difficulty pushing it. Something was not quite adjusted. Lo and behold, the mate turns up. In a few minutes he's sanded down a board and, there, the door is sliding as it should. The job is completed. I'm relieved. What uncalculated good fortune. I'm ever so grateful. On leaving, the mate tosses in, as an impish aside, "No problem, I'm a builder!" He was unpretentious and humble enough not to have mentioned that before. I appreciated a job well done.

All these unexpected kindnesses reinforce words I recall from my return to university studies in 2009-12. Professor George Kent, of the University of Hawaii, was running a course on the "Human Right to Adequate Food". It was part of my Master's in "Peace and Conflict Studies" through Sydney University. The exacting, yet generous Professor insisted, *"What mainly determines health is the degree to which people care about one another's well-being."*

If today, the latter part of 2018, I'm still well and carrying on, after having seemed shattered to smithereens and tested to my very bowels, I would attribute much to the delicate caring of others.

The smallest of kindnesses, a smile, a kind word, a thoughtful act, create, as I see it, stepping stones to peace and harmony. We could remind ourselves of the words of Pope Francis, in his 2016 address on non-violence: "We all desire peace; many people build it each day by little gestures … We can all be craftsmen of peace."

THIRTEEN

A new year – and yet, a closing

Keep thyself as a pilgrim and a guest upon the earth
To whom belongeth nothing of worldly business.
Thomas à Kempis

There's nothing more sobering than to carry in one's arms the ashes of a loved one. Man's return to ashes signifies the end of life's pilgrimage. What is left are memories, the good times and, perhaps, not so good. Nothing material is of any significance. We are just dust. Peace and finality reign. It is beholden on those left to continue life's journey, to respect as best we can, the final wishes of someone departed. Albert wanted to return to the sea. To the underworld of Isle of Pines he loved so much, he knew so well. We had cast most of his ashes into the fast-flowing river at Chekomaria, but his wish was to return to our own island's watery depths. I still had a second little box of ashes. It was my duty to fulfil Albert's wish, to find peace for him.

A Danish friend kept her long-standing promise to visit us over New Year, even though I was now one, not two. Spiritual, discreet, an off-the-track traveller to places such as the Ethiopian plateau, Fogo Cape Verde, and Flores in the Azores, her visit was timely, comforting. We booked a table at the nearby hotel – our number nine we took as a good omen: two nines equal eighteen – 2018. We moved gently into the New Year, under the Southern Cross in a clement, mid-summer night sky.

On the first day of January, one tiny fuchsia rose blooms for Albert. Jetta and I breakfast on summer fruits - pineapple, mango, banana, passion-fruit and home-made yoghurt, take a languorous swim and picnic on the peninsula. We've accorded ourselves two days off, away from holiday-maker crowds. We're preparing mentally for the day we've agreed on – tomorrow. We'll go to Brush Island – the balcony in the sun, 7 kilometres from home.

So often did we take visitors there in the 1980s and '90s - we called it "Albert's office". We'll take Albert there. Not to the beach most frequented by visitors, but to the far southern side of the island, facing the open ocean. We gather multi-hued sprays of bougainvillea from the garden – salmon, mauve, magenta, and my one small rose still fresh from yesterday. The hotel's motor boat drops us inside the reef, on the whitest of sand Albert and I have known so well. Then it heads off with visitors to snorkel further beyond.

Jetta and I are alone in the world with Albert. The way he would have wished. Brush's waters are as beautiful as the paintbox aquamarine they've always been. The tide is high. Our former picnic spot still respected and untouched. Jetta almost steps on a banded, dark yellow and black sea snake. She sees it as a sign of renewal.

We walk determinedly to my planned destination, along the shore to the far side of the island. Tall, dark green pines and grey, wispy iron-barks line the raised banks. I'd had one worry – that the south-east wind would wash the ashes in. But how extraordinary. Today the wind is not at all the usual, prevailing breeze coming off the ocean. Today, for some strange summer reason, it's blowing unusually from the north. In fact it's quite strong, but most conveniently cooperative for our mission. I set the little raffia, ribbon-wrapped box on a slight ledge by the sea, take a photo, undo the red ribbon, move forward a bit and, whoops, I slip down the ledge; all of only 30 centimetres of sand crumbles beneath me, but it makes us laugh, breaking the solemnity. I cast the grey, powdery contents into the calm sea. One part lingers longer, waiting perhaps to catch my rose along with the pink petals we toss, floating bright on the aqua water. The petals stretch out, forming a *Fleuve de Vie*, River of Life, the constellation governing Albert's Celtic astrological sign. It's meant to be. A page has turned. Albert has returned to the sea he loved, the sea he dived into with liberating breaths and wholesomeness. Out into the empty, south-west Pacific Ocean.

Our mission is complete. No-one except us, the sea, the sun, the hot January wind, the white white finest of sand. We round the corner heading back. Some local children have come to play. In the distance a huge cruise ship is anchored at Kuto. Civilisation beckons. We've been in another world.

A memorable, mystic moment – just the three of us.

FOURTEEN

Melodies

Someday I'll wish upon a star
and wake up where the clouds are far behind me.
Judy Garland, film *The Wizard of Oz*

Call it coincidence, fine-tuning, or Irish sixth sense, it's uncanny how fitting melodies strike me, unprompted, in the oddest of places.

I had returned to the hotel in Ubud the night before Albert took wings. The doctor had told me that tomorrow would be the last day. My heart was wrung out, yet weirdly, surrealistically serene. We had tried all avenues to keep Albert with us. But it was not to be.

At about 9 p.m., I had stepped into the familiar hotel restaurant. A Balinese pop trio and singer were entertaining. It was their weekly gig. What were they strumming out? I could not believe my ears. The old, 1973 Bob Dylan classic, "Knock, knock, knocking on Heaven's door"! As if I was their only audience. And what followed? "Everything's gonna be alright". Again their choice seemed directed at me. Uncanny.

Some days later, when I'd spent a few days in Brisbane following Bali, it came time to return to New Caledonia. My heart heavy, I felt as if nothing was real, like a fluttering leaf spiralling down to flat bottom. I dragged one foot in front of the other towards the departure lounge for Noumea. What filtered through the early morning coffee atmosphere? A muted Judy Garland piped through the sound system, lilting from another era, "Somewhere over the rainbow". Was it for me?

Those lyrics from 1939, and familiar to my childhood, continue: "Someday I'll wish upon a star and wake up where the clouds are far behind me, where troubles melt like lemon drops way above the chimney tops that's where you'll find me."

Some ethereal spirit seemed to be carrying me along, as indeed it felt there was no way I could get there on my own.

Awaking on my first day home, I switched on my bedside radio, what did I capture: "Je pense à toi" (I'm thinking of you). As the French say, "Aie, aie aie!" Ouch! Oh my goodness, that echoes my all-invasive, only thought.

It was the first day of August, the day of the memorial ceremony at the village church. I wanted it to be beautiful, dignified, uplifting, not dour and heavy. So, for the entry accompaniment I chose 11 minutes of Dvorak's *New World Symphony,* a recording made by the Saint Petersburg Symphony Orchestra and recorded at Les Folles Journées de Nantes, an annual long weekend music feast. We'd had the chance to visit both cities in recent years and loved each of them. To close the mass, the choir members present joined in a recording by the full Isle of Pines church choir, lifting their voices to Handel's resounding Alleluia – "Sound the trumpets! Let the angels sing!"

Oh God, take care of dear Albert. May he stay by my shoulder, watch over me.

Not all poignant, unsolicited melodies offered comfort. Some echoed distinct discomfort. Early 2018, having run up against the notary I've already mentioned (whom I considered arrogant), American blues cohorts Ben Harper and Charlie Musselwhite warble: "Is there no mercy in this land?" The electric guitar and harmonica pair strike a cord with my feeling that's continued over recent months, as I bang my head against administrative walls, exacerbating my wanting to rail about the same *Monsieur* condescendingly addressing me as *Mademoiselle* – Miss – an old-fashioned term few people use nowadays to address older women, preferring *Madame* out of respect. After all, I'm old enough to be the fellow's mother and who is he to design cast aspersions on my situation?

In a gentler mood, one day the Jazz Groove plays one of Louis Armstrong's less familiar songs, "Summer Song". Its lyrics are worth sharing:

> Love to me is like a Summer's day,
> If it ends, the memories will stay
> still and warm and peaceful.
> Now the days are getting long,
> I can sing my Summer Song.

A friend writes: "Cherish the memories". Cherish. What a beautiful word. And yes, when I look back on our packed years that whizzed by, I savour the cherishing. Our having done so much, rather than just dreaming. Now my mind's library is replete to dream backwards. Now, the latter part of 2018, I've come to the reluctant acceptance that we've each been allotted a certain time on this planet. And that Albert shared half his long life with me.

I switch on the radio, early morning mid-September, the American rock duo, the Rembrandts, sing and strum out: "Baby, That's just the way it is, Baby." I shrug. I guess that's the way it is.

As I write this small chapter, another brother of ours, an industrial chemist, smart, witty, zany, articulate, but sadly, bedevilled, bewitched, beset by a woman, not of our feather, has chosen to leave this life of his own accord. What burst forth from the radio when I learned the news: "Unchain my heart, Set me free". Coincidence? Uncanny Irishness? Whatever. Joe Cocker was formulating our sibling's only way out. The words Beware, Be Wary, could well apply here. But that's another story.

FIFTEEN

Trees and memories

Remember me when I am gone away
Gone far away into the silent land.
Remember, Christina Rossetti

What better, living way to evoke memories than to plant a tree or a shrub, then watch over it, care for it, talk to it as it grows?

Roger's idea, launched in one of the first emails of sympathy I received, has spread and pleases friends by involving themselves in invoking Albert's memory for the future. A *Kunie,* Isle of Pines-born, Melanesian, he exudes a particular empathy with Nature, its meaning and messages, as well as possessing a droll sense of humour, a quick tongue with puns and a rather worldly outlook, having lived outside this little island country (in France actually), for some 20 years.

The native apple tree, pommier-kanak, he planted, struggled at first. "Pomme Tchitchu" he's called it, recalling Albert's island name, "Tchit-chu" for Jesus. For the moment it's a fledgling, but when mature will have fluffy, bright pink flowers and fruit tinged with pink, that from a distance resemble apples, but are more elongated and not as dense as traditional cooler climate apples.

In the rustic Ardennes region of France, 17,000 kilometres away, not far from the Belgian border, another long-time friend, now retired from New Caledonia, spontaneously planted an apple tree in Albert's memory about the same time. A true apple tree this time, and one year later it's flourishing.

The High Chief and his wife like the idea. In fact the tree I've dedicated to Albert in our garden, is a young Kaori, Nini, the High Chief's wife, gave me to plant in 2015. For a long while in its first two years, the sapling took hold but showed little growth. Standing about 30 centimetres high, it vegetated in a nether world of Will I? Won't I? In the past year, however, it's burgeoned and now stands over a metre, its pale green, spear-shaped foliage stretching out, tips turning elegantly skywards. This cousin of the king of New Zealand forests, Kauri, *Agathis australis*, is also an *Agathis*. Conifers, they're part of the Auracaria family, to which belongs Isle of Pines own pine tree, *Araucaria columnaris*. The straight, tall trunk of a mature Kaori in New Caledonia, as the Kauri in northern New Zealand, may reach a height of 50 metres at maturity. Who, I wonder, will check on its development in 40 to 50 years time, cyclones and droughts notwithstanding? Should it survive, I like to think the straight, imposing specimen will be a reflection of the image of one special person who spent a similar time on this beautiful island. Of course I won't be of this world to tell the tale.

A memories patchwork of Albert is being sown together, scattered here and there around the globe. An old Caledonian friend with whom I have a journalist's *entente*, and his friend from Boston, have planted an oak by a lake at their summer house in Quebec, Canada. "It'll one day grow majestic, tall and straight like Albert," they wrote.

In far-eastern Switzerland, not far from Germany and Austria, outside the pretty, old city of St Gallen, a former girlfriend of Albert's, Ursi, planted a 15-year-old fir tree. She bought it from a nursery late 2017. The stocky evergreen's snow-covered, spreading branches made for a picture postcard winter-long. But come summer this year, 2018, prolonged dry throughout Europe did not appeal to the mountain resident. It browned up and battled to survive. Now Ursi's giving it another winter to try to settle in to its new home and thrive as it should – a link with Isle of Pines and with a long friendship.

A French/Japanese couple, from rural Auvergne in the heart of France, who spent more than a decade on Isle of Pines, proposes planting a Japanese maple for both of us, recalling how we loved visiting Japan. Much of the reason for our regular visits over 30 years was Albert's oldest brother being a missionary in the far north of Iwate-ken. A vocation he espoused for some 50 years. The Japanese maple, whose foliage turns bright orange in autumn, should do well in the healthy Auvergnat climate at some 300 metres altitude. In the language of flowers, it's said to symbolise reserve and a free spirit. The elegant species, lauded in paintings, given its delicate, wispy foliage, couldn't be more aptly chosen.

Far away, on the other side of the world, in the eastern Pacific, on Huahine island in Tahiti, a long-time friend (with whom we organised some of the first cruise ship calls to Isle of Pines in the mid '80s) and his artist-painter wife, say they can't go past planting the emblematic shrub, Tahiti Tiaré. Part of the gardenia family, the highly-perfumed flower represents all that's exotic in that fabled island archipelago. This white, star-shaped flower is not just something to be recalled in Gauguin paintings, but is rather a charm incorporated into everyday life throughout Tahiti – flower garlands and hair garnish, the perfume of soaps and oils, the evocative scent that hangs in the air. Little wonder, in the language of flowers, the Tahiti Tiaré is associated with romanticism and love.

Back in our part of the Pacific, nearly 5000 kilometres further west as the crow flies, or five hours separation as planes fly, in Noumea, Gigi and Roland offered to plant a rose. A few doors along the same street, other old friends have planted a rare, blue hibiscus. The unusual hybrid is Eric and Christine's reminder of Albert outside their kitchen door at the foot of their steep-slope garden in an older suburb of Noumea. They watch over the struggling slip of a plant that had a hard time surviving the months-long drought that beset all of New Caledonia until late January 2018. So brittle was the countryside in the whole country that people on our island considered renouncing the traditional yam harvest always held in March, for want of lack of growth, the tubers not being worth harvesting for that specific date.

Italian-French Vincent and his wife and two littlies, wrote in September a year ago, that they'd ceremoniously planted an olive tree in their garden in Noumea. Albert, whose mother came from Modena, Italy, loved olive oil – a small flask stood on our table, alongside the salt and pepper mills, at lunch and dinner everyday. Meanwhile, Martine, Vincent's mother, who lives on the Mediterranean island, Elba, has planted a fig tree. Evocative of biblical times and on traditional, arid ground common to the region, the fig tree for Albert will hopefully mature in an area not unlike Isle of Pines – a diver's haven of turquoise waters. Elba, off the Tuscan coast was also an island of exile – famously for having sheltered Napoleon for almost a year after his forced abdication in 1814.

Back on our island, in June 2018, one of the island's apiarists stops by our house to deliver honey. He tells me he's planted a lime tree in Albert's memory. "It's doing well," he says. Kindness, thoughtfulness again.

Symbolic, revered in Melanesian culture, the *bugny*, planted in full ceremony the first day of August a year ago, at Nataiwatch, has now taken hold. As has the indigenous Araucaria pine that Nataiwatch's owner, Guillaume, planted on his tribal land further north on the island.

Flourishing too, is the coconut tree our three photographer friends from Noumea planted that same August afternoon. Fourteen months later, one of them, Pierre-Alain, checks on their memorial when visiting for a few days. A sensitive man, he strokes a top leaf. "I chose a coconut tree", he explains, "because it's feminine in Melanesian culture. As you know, Albert loved women." True. Albert was pro-women, an admirer, a collaborator, a friend. He respected women. Perhaps it went back to the influence of his dignified Italian mother, a woman well with her husband, a good and loving mother, a hard worker and an excellent cook. Dusnelda was her name.

The latest grandchild in the close Croatian family I lived with as a student in New York State, has another unusual name -- Linden. Albert was welcomed into the family, just as I had been many years previously. I write asking if they'll consider planting a linden tree, *tilleul,* in French. We were struck by the impressive linden trees in the grounds of a wonderful, Renzo Piano-designed art gallery, Fondation Beyeler in Basel, Switzerland. The gallery celebrates Monet's renowned waterlilies, reaching out into the gardens; the linden trees stand grand, close by. And summer in Montreux, Switzerland, we remembered the steep street leading to the old village carpeted with tufts of distinctive, perfumed linden flowers.

Early October 2018, Pierre-Emmanuel who now runs the scuba-diving business, Kunie Scuba Center, of which our Nauticlub, was the forerunner, pulls a sapling *Cerisier de Cayenne*, a Cayenne or Creole cherry as it's called in English, from under the bush laden with bright red fruit, in front of our boutique. Fitting that he offers to plant it in the scuba diving centre's newly cleared garden at the north of the island, in memory of Albert.

Meaningful, participatory actions such as planting a tree, a shrub or a flowering plant, remembering someone close, have, in Albert's case, replaced the ritualised custom-giving in Melanesian society, so respected here. Paying respects for a bereavement on our island mostly involves gifts of the heavy, yam tuber, foodstuffs such as kilos of white sugar, rice and cooking oil, and bolts of colourful, island floral material into which is slipped a bill or bills of paper money. The gestures in Albert's memory patchwork remain living, ongoing, perpetuating a touch of hope, expectation and surprise. He would be the first to be surprised, honoured, delighted.

SIXTEEN

More roses

"… it is the peculiar power of flowers, that while they are universal and spread their species over the world, they invoke in each beholder the dearest and most cherished memories".

The Small Miracle, Paul Gallico

Planting a flower or flowering bush is potentially not as enduring as planting trees. Nevertheless, floral species possess an evocative power that escapes some trees.

I've kept mentioning our little fuchsia rose and it's following me, it's blooming often, at significant moments. I cannot find the name of this simple rose. I'd define it as an old-fashioned, garden, miniature, almost wild rose.

"All miniatures," wrote rose expert, Stirling Macoboy of Neutral Bay, Sydney, "descend from Rouletti, something of a mystery rose. In the early 1800s," he explained, "miniature forms of the already diminutive China Roses appeared, introduced, it was said, from Mauritius. They became fashionable pot plants for decorating window-sills, particularly in Paris, but … the fashion died out." Perhaps it's Fringette that Macoboy first saw in Vienna, in the Belvedere Palace alpine garden, "where only the most diminutive of flowers are admitted." It has 25 deep pink petals, exactly as scattered on one of the pages of his book, exactly as adorn my garden sparingly, from time to time, exactly as I gathered each day in Ubud to take to Albert.

Last year's drought meant that I could give my frail rose bushes no more than a drop of water, morning and night. They bore few blooms.

As the feast days 1 November (All Saints' Day) and 2 November (All Souls' Day) approached, a team of village women tidied the cemetery. One of them told me the amaryllis lily, *hippeastrum,* that she had planted at the head of Albert's spot had flowered. (The idea of living flowers enhancing a tomb is, to me, far more appealing than everlasting, lifeless plastic ones.)

Every day, leading up to 1 November, when I'd promised myself I'd make the pilgrimage to Albert on my own, I would watch for a new rose bud. Come the day, I rise before six, gather my hiker's stick, some water, camera (until then I hadn't the courage to take photos up there), and lo, my garden provides me with two tiny fuchsia roses. A red ribbon to knot them together. I climb the hill behind the church in the freshness of early morning. A dozen or so cars indicate worshippers are inside for six o'clock mass, one of two services today, when all public services and businesses are closed in New Caledonia (as in France). Whether the bulk of the population does any more than lie-in and luxuriate in a day off, mid-week, is open to discussion. But it is common that people remember loved ones in cemeteries today, visiting, flowering and honouring their graves, today being a holiday (*Toussaint*), rather than tomorrow, when it's back to work (although that is officially *La Fête des Morts*, All Souls' Day, as we know it in English). I'm almost alone in the peaceful cemetery.

On leaving, I hear voices and a smatter of laughter. I meet two Kunie women, one who lost her husband mid-year too. Melanie hugs me, calms my tears and talks soothingly of her husband and of Tchitchu, Albert's local nickname, dating from his early years on Isle of Pines, when, tall, slender, long-haired, bearded, he decidedly resembled the image often associated with Jesus. He walked or rode a horse. The nickname seemed to fit.

From then on, early November, almost no roses bloomed in my garden. Come New Year's Day, 2018, there was one, just one rose on its slender stem. I picked it to grace our kitchen bar. The next day I looked for another. No. The one in the vase was the only one. It had a special mission, for Brush Island, as I related in Chapter 13. The prolonged drought meant there were no more little blooms, till, could I be so fortunate, 14 February – yes, St. Valentine's Day.

My small rose is not the only one that keeps Albert's memory alive. Nor is it the only rose that behaves as if it possesses a spiritual cord of empathy. Joëlle, a long-time friend living in the Queensland hinterland, planted a more sophisticated, deep red rose, called "rose jewel", shortly after our memorial ceremony. It didn't seem happy where it was, so she re-potted and re-positioned it. I visited her in late March this year, and, believe it or not, the rose bloomed its first deep-red head the day I arrived. The almost life-like sensitivity doesn't end there. After spending two weeks in the area, Joëlle then took me to the train station. Believe it or not, when she arrived home, she found rose petals scattered on her terrace. The rose that had stayed in bloom those two weeks had been shorn off mid-stem! Not a phantom's hand, but the beady eye and swift dash of a cheeky white, yellow-crested cockatoo! Did he connive with my departure?

On Isle of Pines, one of the women vendors at our twice-weekly village market has planted another deep-red remembrance rose, this one a grander size. Mid-year, Aurélie, who brings a basket of produce she has in the garden, green coconuts to drink, bananas, flowers, carambole (star fruit), tells me to her surprise, that her rose has already bloomed once. Albert, you're not forgotten.

Felicity, my sister, and her husband Georges, who also live in Queensland, planted a yellow rose. It wasn't doing well. And she doesn't have "green fingers". They repotted and re-positioned it. Lo and behold, come 30 June, Albert's first anniversary, it bloomed, not just one, but two exquisite, plump, golden yellow blooms.

Friends from Noumea delivered by hand a card featuring a delicate, old-fashioned painted rose, the same as mine. Its poignant verse, "The Rose Beyond the Wall", reads:

"A rose once grew where all could see, sheltered beside a garden wall, And, as the days passed swiftly by, it spread its branches, straight and tall ... One day a beam of light shone through a crevice that had opened wide - The rose bent gently toward its warmth then passed beyond to the other side...

"Now, you who deeply feel its loss, be comforted – the rose blooms there - its beauty even greater now, nurtured by God's own loving care."

Such sentiments could verge on the maudlin and pathetic, were it not for Macoboy, in the introduction to his encyclopedic work, pointedly reminding us:

"... what about the thorny branches?

Perhaps they are the rose's final grace, the flaw that saves it from that too great a perfection that we mortals can only admire, but not really love."

SEVENTEEN

In praise of the iPad

*There are six billion people in this world
And it makes me feel quite small,
'cos you're the one I love the most of all.*

Katie Melua

None of this story would have unfolded as it did without the complicity of one amazing item of technology, measuring only 14 x 21 centimetres. My iPad became my sophisticated, mobile office. Outside the one, fruitless phone call I made to the travel insurance base in France, and the equally fruitless call I received from the honorary German consulate in Sanur, my iPad was my only communication with the world within and without Bali.

I blessed Steves Job and Wozniak for their company's (Apple) inventiveness, their practicality. Had the same situation arisen ten years earlier, I cannot imagine how I would have coped. How would I have been able to inform our far-flung families? How would I have been able to keep them in touch with daily updates? Then with the ultimate end and the beginning of a whole new situation to circumnavigate, how could I have been so fortunate that my youngest brother would fly to my side? Within a few hours, I learned that he had booked a ticket and would fly the six hours Brisbane to Bali and would arrive at the appointed time late at night.

How could I have obtained medical history from New Caledonia or received and informed the Saba hospital doctors of various reports? How could I have arranged the multitude of payments I was beset with, without their being able to make their way through the international banking wavelengths. Postal mail would have taken weeks, perhaps months. Without payment, I would have been captured and marooned in Bali.

Skype via iPad made for more personalised contact with friends and family. Comfort and commiseration rolled into one. A whole world for a few weeks reduced to an A5 rectangle. It contained too, our last happy photos. That same portable, condensed computer became my mailbox for messages of condolence and sympathy when Albert slipped "to the other side". In the space of a whizz and a whirr it put me in contact with friends and family in England, France, Switzerland, the States, New Zealand, Australia and Japan.

I was coming home without the one I loved the most of all. My iPad wrapped up many of the details. Yes, I felt decidedly small.

EIGHTEEN

Days ahead

He who is wise in his heart, sorrows neither for the living nor the dead.

All that lives, lives for ever. Only the shell, the perishable, passes away.

The spirit is without end, eternal, death-less.

The Bhagavad-Gita

One day mid-July 2018, more than a year later, I shake myself, admonish myself, and admit we, each human being, has apparently each been given an allotted time on earth.

Albert made the most of his time. He never frittered it away. He worked hard, he enjoyed his days, he relished relaxation, as he relished candles, a well-set table gracing good meals and a glass or three. He planned and realised his plans, his dreams. His was a life well-filled.

I don't know that I'm wise. But I do know that the past year has taught me much. That after a mournful, sickening *annus horribilus*, I can now say to myself, perhaps I've still some allotted days left. Best I make the most of them. Put into them what I can. Share. Keep a little curiosity, an opening for a glimmer of surprise. As a bird with a broken wing, I may learn to fly again, differently.

Continue life's path with me, *mon chéri*. Keep me company all the way.

Reference Works

Baum, Vicki, *Love and Death in Bali,* 1937, Tuttle Publishing 1999

Gallico, Paul, *The Small Miracle,* Michael Joseph Ltd, 1951

Gibran, Kahlil, *The Prophet,* William Heinemann Ltd, 1923, 1972

Harari, Yuval Noah, *21 Lessons for the 21st Century,* Spiegel & Grau, New York, 2018

LaValley, Barry, *So You Think You are Ready to Retire?,* Retirement Lifestyle Center Inc., 2014

Macoboy, Stirling, *Macoboy's ROSES,* Mallon Publishing, 1997

Mason, Diana, *The Force of Life, in the anthology Beyond Expectations, fourteen New Zealand women write about their lives,* Allen & Unwin, 1986

Murakami, Haruki, *What I Talk About When I Talk About Running,* Alfred A. Knopf, New York, 2008

O'Donohue, John, *Anam Cara, Spiritual Wisdom from the Celtic World,* Bantam Books, 1997

Pope Francis, *World Message on Non-Violence,* 8th December, 2016

www.ingramcontent.com/pod-product-compliance
Lightning Source LLC
Chambersburg PA
CBHW041926090426
42743CB00020B/3451